# Poetry Motion

# Dorset

### Edited by Lynsey Hawkins

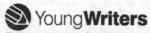 Young**Writers**

First published in Great Britain in 2004 by:
Young Writers
Remus House
Coltsfoot Drive
Peterborough
PE2 9JX
Telephone: 01733 890066
Website: www.youngwriters.co.uk

SB ISBN 1 84460 345 8

# Foreword

This year, the Young Writers' 'Poetry In Motion' competition proudly presents a showcase of the best poetic talent selected from over 40,000 up-and-coming writers nationwide.

Young Writers was established in 1991 to promote the reading and writing of poetry within schools and to the youth of today. Our books nurture and inspire confidence in the ability of young writers and provide a snapshot of poems written in schools and at home by budding poets of the future.

The thought effort, imagination and hard work put into each poem impressed us all and the task of selecting poems was a difficult but nevertheless enjoyable experience.

We hope you are as pleased as we are with the final selection and that you and your family continue to be entertained with *Poetry In Motion Dorset* for many years to come.

# Contents

| | |
|---|---|
| Emily Francis  (13) | 19 |
| Ellena Kapoor  (13) | 20 |
| Carl Kill  (13) | 20 |
| Teshany Perrett-Conn  (13) | 21 |
| David Charlston  (14) | 21 |
| Aaron Revel  (13) | 22 |
| Rochelle Drew  (15) | 23 |
| Christopher Danvers  (13) | 24 |
| Laura Birch  (13) | 25 |
| Loren Dowding  (13) | 26 |
| Anna Tabrah  (13) | 26 |
| Naomi Pearce  (13) | 27 |
| David Hoyland  (13) | 27 |
| Kimberley Inman  (14) | 28 |
| Rebecca Clarke  (13) | 29 |

## Cranborne County Middle School

| | |
|---|---|
| Sarah Froud  (12) | 30 |
| Annaliese Allcock  (11) | 30 |
| Ellie Killeen  (11) | 31 |
| Laura House  (11) | 31 |
| Clayton Godfrey | 32 |
| Katie Kynaston  (11) | 32 |
| Sophie Court  (12) | 33 |
| Libby Bell  (11) | 34 |

## Oakmead College of Technology

| | |
|---|---|
| Matthew Macdonald  (12) | 34 |
| Lauren Clark  (12) | 35 |
| Mack Bishop  (11) | 35 |
| Courtney Esson  (12) | 36 |
| Charmaine Slaughter  (12) | 37 |
| Hayley Goddard  (12) | 38 |
| Sam Reagen  (12) | 38 |
| Jack Holmes  (12) | 39 |
| Hannah Boyce  (13) | 40 |
| Siobhan Hiscock  (12) | 41 |
| Sophie Lawrence  (13) | 42 |
| Sherry Lumber  (12) | 43 |
| Kristie Henley  (12) | 44 |
| Helen McCann  (11) | 45 |

## Parkstone Grammar School

| | |
|---|---|
| Anna Stone  (12) | 72 |
| Melissa Elsworth  (12) | 73 |
| Claire Constantine  (13) | 73 |
| Nicola Beattie  (12) | 74 |
| Hazel Wallace  (14) | 74 |
| Charli Watkins  (12) | 75 |
| Amy Sparrow  (13) | 75 |
| Rosie Browne  (12) | 76 |
| Sarah Maiden  (12) | 76 |
| Philippa Rook  (12) | 77 |
| Hannah Elder  (12) | 77 |
| Fiona Wall  (12) | 78 |
| Dannielle Cox  (12) | 78 |
| Leanne Columbine  (13) | 79 |
| Stacey Osmond  (13) | 79 |
| Bryony Greenfield  (14) | 80 |
| Emma Porter  (12) | 80 |
| Emma Guy  (14) | 81 |
| Tiggy Burrows  (12) | 81 |
| Katie Morris  (14) | 82 |
| Kirsty Gurney  (13) | 83 |
| Hannah Waring  (13) | 84 |
| Anna Ramsbottom  (12) | 85 |
| Lizzie Wheable  (12) | 85 |
| Elizabeth Jackson  (13) | 86 |
| Lauren Curley  (16) | 87 |
| Alicia Wright  (12) | 88 |
| Jodie Elmer  (12) | 89 |
| Natasha Scotson  (12) | 90 |
| Emily Knights  (13) | 91 |

**Portchester School**

| | |
|---|---|
| Dave Hunter  (15) | 92 |
| Marco Goisis  (14) | 92 |
| Matt Roberts  (14) | 93 |
| Ryan Head  (16) | 94 |
| Nathan Dawes  (14) | 95 |
| Christian Meade  (14) | 95 |
| Thomas Daubney  (12) | 96 |
| Lee-Paul Chapman  (15) | 96 |
| David Harvey  (14) | 97 |

| | |
|---|---:|
| Jonathan Mills (14) | 175 |
| Emma Bartlett (15) | 175 |
| Katie Creevy (15) | 176 |
| Jenny Ricketts (13) | 176 |
| Guy Adams (14) | 177 |
| Alex Middleditch (14) | 177 |
| Jessica Owens (13) | 178 |
| Jennie Bird (14) | 178 |
| Sarah-Jane Foster (15) | 179 |
| James Creevy (12) | 179 |
| Rhiannon Wilson (13) | 180 |
| Oscar Weiner (13) | 180 |
| Tom Nicolet (14) | 181 |
| Toby Hoare (12) | 181 |
| Charlie Power (13) | 182 |
| Fleur Ruddick (13) | 182 |
| Emily Daniels (12) | 183 |
| Chloe Everett (13) | 183 |
| Anastasia Hernandez Beaumont (12) | 184 |
| Onari Tariah (12) | 184 |
| Sam Breslin (15) | 185 |
| Tim Johnson (11) | 186 |
| Peter Gordon (11) | 187 |
| Molly Bradshaw (12) | 188 |
| Amy Gollings (11) | 189 |
| Oliver Hoare (11) | 190 |
| Jonathan Cooper (12) | 191 |
| Jack Kane (13) | 192 |
| Nabil Mahmoud (13) | 193 |
| Roxanne Coulstock (11) | 194 |
| Peter Dixon (13) | 195 |
| Piers Bate (13) | 196 |
| Alexander Boucouvalas (14) | 197 |
| Thomas Hawkins (11) | 198 |
| Terry Baskett (11) | 199 |
| William Brown (11) | 200 |
| Alanna Hamilton (12) | 200 |
| Jace Latore (14) | 201 |
| Abigail Langley (13) | 202 |
| Jack Hayter (13) | 203 |
| Louis Hashtroudi (11) | 204 |
| Tristan Breslin (12) | 205 |

Harriet Tombs  (12)                                    205
Bethany Williams  (11)                                 206
Andrew Houlder  (11)                                   206
William Smith  (11)                                    206
Christina Guerra-Unwin  (11)                           207
James Smith  (11)                                      207
Shadman Chowdhury  (10)                                207
Christian Bulpitt  (12)                                208
Byron Russell  (10)                                    208
Dale Beesley  (10)                                     209

## Wentworth College
Rebecca Galton  (14)                                   209
Pippa Janssenswillen  (13)                             210

# The Poems

# Respecting The Respectful - Rejection

How he longed to walk free of this life,
to run with the wind in his face.
These lifelong chains holding him back,
treated like a different race.

How he longed to walk free of this life,
to play and have friends of his own.
To gain independence and feel normal too,
to be able to wander and roam.

How he longed to walk free of this life,
to enjoy the pleasures boys do.
To reminisce of his first ever kiss,
to be a somebody, not what or a who.

**Louise Brown  (15)**
**Avonbourne Business & Enterprise College**


# Missing You

Missing you is so easy
When you're not there, it's so hard
Out of the pain
That we are now in
I can still hear you in my thoughts
Still picture you in my mind
Your presence lingers in the air
Yet your body has been taken away
I seem to be the only one
That knows you're still here
You're beside me, I can feel you
Stay near me, though absent.

**Charlotte Leech  (15)**
**Avonbourne Business & Enterprise College**

# Thoughts

Thoughts can be feelings,
Thoughts can be words,
Thoughts can be nothing at all,
But thoughts must be something,
Because otherwise they don't exist.

Thoughts are something inside your head,
That spins round and round,
They make you dizzy sometimes,
They can make you sad,
They can make you as light as air.

They can give you nightmares,
They can give exciting dreams,
They can swirl round your head,
As fast as fast can be,
But sometimes they stop.

Then when you wake they start again,
What are these thoughts in your head,
That swirl and spin round?
Could they be words or feelings,
Or just nothing at all?

But they must be something,
Otherwise why are they there?
To buzz round your head,
To confuse you day and night,
Or to help you speak the right words.

I do wonder why they are here,
Thoughts that could be feelings,
Thoughts that could be words,
Thoughts that might not even be there,
Thoughts inside my head.

**Sophie Wettstein (11)**
**Avonbourne Business & Enterprise College**

# Jesus

He was born in a stable
In a cattle shed
He was born to be able
To save us all

They were on a fishing boat
When up rose a storm
They wondered would it float
Or would they feel forlorn?

He died on a cross
On a Friday morn
He was such a loss
They shouted with scorn

He rose again
On the third day
Was He real then?
People wished He would stay.

**Natalie Acreman  (11)**
**Avonbourne Business & Enterprise College**


# A Deserted Beach

The waves crashed against the slippery rocks,
The breeze swept through my tasselled locks,
The seagulls screeched a sudden cry,
On where they flew through the midnight sky,
The moon cast shadows upon the shore,
The waves leapt high, on the rocks they tore,
The sky as black as hard burnt toast,
As the sea moved in towards the coast
And silence lay across the beach,
As the seagulls made their last night screech.

**Louise Carter  (11)**
**Avonbourne Business & Enterprise College**

# The Mysterious Cat . . .

One afternoon,
I was watching TV,
When there was a knock on the door,
It startled me.

I opened the door
And on the mat,
Sat the most amazing cat.

Its eyes were green and gleaming at me,
Its coat was as black as it could be.

'May I come in?' the cat announced,
Before I could speak,
In he pounced.

He ran in the kitchen and said, 'I want food,'
I followed him in and thought,
'How rude!'

I said to the cat,
'Don't you mean please?'
'Sorry,' he said,
'Do you have some cheese?'

I gave him some in a little dish
And now the cat had got his wish,
He licked his paws and wiped his ears
And in a flash -
He disappeared.

**Grace Nevill  (11)**
**Avonbourne Business & Enterprise College**

# You Don't Get Me

I don't think you get what it's like to be me,
To look through my eyes, to see what I see.
I don't think you get the pain I have felt,
The hurt and the sadness which I have been dealt.

I don't think you get what I have been through
And the admiration I feel when I look at you.
I don't think you get my hopes and my dreams,
How this person you know, isn't all that she seems.

I don't think you get my terror and my tears,
To walk in my footsteps, to know my fears,
I don't think you get my secrets untold,
To know my misfortunes, my heart to behold.

I don't think you get what life's like for me,
You don't even want to, that's how it must be.
I don't think you get what it's like to be me,
To look through my eyes, you can't see what I see.

**Kathryn McStraw (14)**
**Avonbourne Business & Enterprise College**

# My Love Is Like A Bright Red Rose

My heart is like a candle
That's sweetly lit at night
I use it when it is dark
'Cause it shines so very bright

My love is like a bright red rose
That's newly grown in June
My love is like the melody
That's dearly played in tune.

**Ellinor Utbult (11)**
**Avonbourne Business & Enterprise College**

# A Pirate's Tale

Sailing the seven seas,
Would be a brilliant life for me,
With a hip ho ho and a bottle of rum,
Being a pirate would be so much fun.

Secret islands of silver and gold,
Where in our minds we would never get old,
With a down you go take a sword and a gun,
Being a pirate would be so much fun.

With the big blue horizon as far as the eye can see,
It's all so perfect, a pirate's life for me,
With an all's right captain in the rain and sun,
Being a pirate would be so much fun.

Travelling freely where our souls decide,
Being on a boat - before our dreams collide,
With a take-no-prisoners, be sure to stun,
Being a pirate would be so much fun.

No rules, no laws to abide by,
No kings or governors to test or try,
With a we'll have a party take every crumb,
Being a pirate would be so much fun.

**Hannah Green  (13)**
**Avonbourne Business & Enterprise College**

# Antarctica!

The bitter wind howling,
The polar bear growling,
The snow gently falling,
The baby seals calling.

The snow softly scattering,
Human's teeth chattering,
Glaciers slowly breaking,
Whales quietly waking.

The icy waters flowing,
The morning sun glowing,
Polar bears swiftly walking,
Humans quietly stalking.

The snow soft and white,
The moon glowing at night,
The polar bear's bright eyes,
The clear blue skies.

**Jodie Radulovitch  (12)**
**Avonbourne Business & Enterprise College**


# The Little Folks' Festival

Light, delicate and beautiful,
I shall dance at the little folks' festival.

See the rosy berries made ready for the feast
And I shall bring some almond blossoms to make myself a wreath.

From under the starlit sky,
The little folk gather to dance with I.

Around the glen we shall joyfully prance,
So come with I, join the pixies' dance.

**Laura Tomlinson  (11)**
**Bovington Middle School**

# I Am

I am . . .
>  the rotten shed
>  that no longer shelters;
>  the slugs and beasts
>  that eat the plants;
>  the weeds
>  that are like a wicked jungle.

I am . . .
>  the three-legged chair
>  that people still sit on;
>  the mucky pond
>  that is a graveyard to animals;
>  the rust barbecue
>  that no longer lights.

I am . . .
>  the tattered gazebo
>  that has holes the size of footballs;
>  the brown grass
>  that is like poison to creatures;
>  the clothes line
>  that is going to collapse with it gets tapped.

**Peter Kingsland**
**Bovington Middle School**


# Sad I Am

I am . . .
>  The slug that lays on its back;
>  The gazebo that's no longer waterproof;
>  The pond that now is a cemetery;
>  The oily, rotten, old barbecue in the grass;
>  The grey grass that looks old-looking;
>  The lawnmower that spits rusty metal when started.

**Jamie Voaden**
**Bovington Middle School**

# Sad I Ams

I am . . .
The dryness of the grass.
The rust on the clothes line.
The none swinging gazebo.

I am . . .
The dirt on the mouldy shed.
The dust on the barbecue.
The mould on the pond.

I am . . .
The rust bolts of the lawnmower.
The crusty old fence.
The undug flower patch.

I am . . .
The patch overgrown with weeds.
The slug sliding along.
The lichen and hedge-trimmer.

**Jetisse Summers  (12)**
**Bovington Middle School**

# Imagine

If there were no more cats in the world
I would miss
The cuddly faces that hop up to greet me
The miaows and purrs of emotion, the cold-padded paws
The tiny pinpricks of its claws and its warm cuddly face
If there were no more cats in the world
I would miss
The fun of playing, laughing
Their greedy kitten appetite
Happiness would be gone forever
If there were no more cats in the world.

**Kyle Kelly  (12)**
**Bovington Middle School**

# Brazil

The beat of a drum comes into motion,
People shout and cause commotion,
The carnival of Brazil has begun,
The rainforest of Brazil has come alive again.

Fancy costumes roll down the street,
People shake to the rhythm of the beat,
Gold shines through the crowd,
The music plays nice and loud.

Jewellery rattles, tickles and shakes,
The residents complain of the noise it makes,
The night is coming to an end,
It's time for Brazil to finish her trend.

**Brienne Fillingham-Bathie  (12)**
**Bovington Middle School**


# Imagine

If there were no more cats in the world,
I would miss,
The warm fur tickling my fingers,
The big eyes staring at you
Through their two slices of skin,
The long, sharp claws digging into your flesh,
The small, furry tongue licking your hand,
The long, swishing tail,
Imagine a world in which there were no more cats.

**Jasmine Donnelly  (12)**
**Bovington Middle School**

# I Am A Garden!

I am a garden that . . .
Doesn't know the meaning of weeds,
Always full of life and good deeds.
I am a garden that . . .
Is a house-dog and everyone cares,
No need to scavenge or do bad dares.
I am a garden that . . .
Is a TV guide, so I'm never put down,
It's like I'm royalty, with a crown.
I am a garden that . . .
Is a pencil case, always needed to store things,
I'm always in use, it's like I'm with kings.
I am a garden that . . .
Is a classroom, that is full of kids,
I'm never covered, especially from lids.
I am a garden that . . .
Is never neglected,
I'm always respected!

**Ryan Donald  (12)**
**Bovington Middle School**


# I Am A Garden

I am a garden bright and merry
A little flower blooms upon a red berry
I am a garden full of sun
I'm joyful and bright till the day is done
I am a garden that when I go dark
I still hear the sound of a puppy bark
I am a garden, sunny you'll see
I always have been and I always will be.

**Sophie Miller  (12)**
**Bovington Middle School**

# Don't Worry

Don't worry you're fine
You're in a hospital that's divine.
When you're treated to the best of care,
Just remember the love and care.
When you're feeling down in the dumps,
Don't make yourself feel like a lump.
A little jab will make you feel much better,
So play a game to make you feel better.
When you think about a dove,
It makes you feel as if you're loved.
If you are having an operation,
They will give you plenty of information.
Get a doctor if you feel bad,
Just remember not to be so sad.
When you want to play,
Just say!
When someone's feeling down,
Just take them for a good look around.
If you feel as if you have had a fright,
Close your eyes real tight -
When you have got nothing to say,
Just go off and play.
If you want to read a book,
Get one about good looks!
When a monster enters your dreams,
Think about your favourite ice cream.
When you think about the weather,
Just get yourself together.
If you felt alone,
Just go and play with the phone.
When you have had enough,
Get someone who's really tough.
When you think it's time for bed,
Get someone to bring you a final piece of bread.
When you feel as if you're hurt,
Go and tell a person on alert.

When you are at Great Ormond Street,
Just think of the great people that you will meet.
You will feel just at home,
Don't complain about going home!
It's always going to be a little bit frightening,
So I wouldn't think a lot about scary, flashy lightning,
When a doctor comes near,
Don't fill yourself up with fear.
Have a really fantastic and brilliant time at hospital!

**Alice McKaigg  (10)**
**Bovington Middle School**


# Spirit

I sometimes feel I'm always trapped,
As if I'm guided by a map.
I'd like the spirit of a wild horse,
I'd like my feet to tread off this course.
I'd like the wolf inside me strong,
I'd like my heart to sing a song.
I'd like to hear the phoenix sing,
I'd like to fly on pure white wings.
I'd like to walk under waterfalls,
I'd like to hear the eagle's calls.
I'd like to see the sun shine down,
I'd like a smile, not a frown.
I feel I'd like to run away,
I'll find the key to my life someday.
I need to reach for that wonderful dream,
Or I fear my soul will forever scream.

**Elizabeth Levett  (12)**
**Bovington Middle School**

# I Am A Garden

I am a garden that everyone loves
Children play happily in me
Even in winter when all wear hats
And fuzzy warm gloves

I am like a beautiful flower that grows in God's garden
I have plants growing all over me
With not a barren area on me
Apart from the ground under the eucalyptus tree

I am like a cool blue swimming pool
I have a shady area where you can sit and think in me
And a fountain where you can drink from.

**Steven Rash  (12)**
**Bovington Middle School**


# A Garden's Lament

I am a garden whose life is destroyed,
No new life will grow here again,
I am a garden whose life is at an end.

I am a garden that absorbs no water,
For the wall that shields me from the rain
Is as cruel as the people who forget me.

I am a garden which will shrivel up
And forever cease to exist.

**Alistair Attwood  (13)**
**Bovington Middle School**


# I'm A Garden

I am a garden combed neatly with flowers!
A library book never put down for hours!
A stray homed and made family!
I am a garden full of possibility!

**Becci McNeill**
**Bovington Middle School**

# Imagine

If there were no more dogs in the world,
I would miss . . .
The shiny sparkle of their big round eyes,
The chewing noise of their bones,
The soft fur rubbing against my leg which makes me look like him,
If there were no more dogs in the world,
I would miss . . .
The sound of the bark that they make,
The big paw lifting up and pulling my arm,
The way they run and never stop,
Imagine the world in which there were no more dogs.

**Dale Hughes**
**Bovington Middle School**


# Sad I Am

I am . . .
    the barbecue with no gas
    the picnic table with snapped planks
    the flowers that no longer have bright petals
    the pots that have been smashed by the frost
    the tree that has come out of the ground
    the rotten shed with smashed glass
    the bark chippings all over the patio.

**Ben Harris**
**Bovington Middle School**


# Garden

I am a garden soon to die,
That has been swept down in its prime,
By gallons and gallons of intoxicated rain
Pouring down from the sky up high,
I am a garden soon to die.

**Joshua Secretan (13)**
**Bovington Middle School**

# Imagine A World

If there were no more dogs in the world,
I would miss . . .
The fluffy paws that rest on my leg when she is begging,
The dark brown eyes that let me know how she is feeling,
The long, skinny legs that spread all over the field
As she goes to fetch the ball,
If there were no more dogs in the world,
I would miss . . .
The long, wet tongue that greets you when you get home,
The quiet yelp when they get hurt,
The waggy tails that smack on your legs,
The constant slobber from the jaws,
Imagine a world in which there were no more dogs . . .

**Zoe Chubb**
**Bovington Middle School**


# Candle In The Window!

A candle flickers with dancing flames,
The draughty window is playing games.

Outside, the wind is very chill,
Inside, the fire crackles still.

The logs are burning very bright,
They cut through the dark of night.

The shadow flickers across the ground,
Until the flame is burning down.

**Abigail Butcher  (11)**
**Bovington Middle School**

# Forgotten

I'm standing there all alone,
Looking for a friend,
Waiting there on my own,
Waiting for this to end.

I look around, dare not move,
Someone's sure to find me,
I turn around, my luck's improved,
There's someone there behind me!

It's a woman from over that road,
She must have seen me here
And wondered why I'm all alone
And trembling with fear.

She asks me why no one's here,
I don't know what to say,
Why was I trembling with fear
In this open alleyway?

**Megan Meaney  (13)**
**Corfe Hills School**


# If Everyone Stopped To Think

If the world is meant to be a safe place,
Why do they make families fear each day and night?
If the world is meant to be a safe place,
Why do they make families have to hide?

If everyone is meant to respect each other,
Why do they choose to mess up people's lives?
If everyone is meant to respect each other,
Why do they tear people's hearts in two?

Some say it doesn't matter what people think,
They will do as they please, no matter what,
But if everyone just stopped to think,
The world would be a better place.

**Lauren Tellier  (13)**
**Corfe Hills School**

# Books

There are lots of different books,
Big ones, small ones, fat ones, thin ones.
Ones with big writing, ones with tiny writing,
Some with pictures, some without,
Some are comedy, others romance.

There are some intended for adults
And some intended for children.
There are lots of different genres,
Comedy, romance, thriller, animal
There is something for everyone.

Most people only read one type,
Like a specific author or genre,
Next time you pick up a book,
Stop and think awhile,
There might be a better book down another aisle.

**Hayley Dyer  (13)**
**Corfe Hills School**


# If I

If I don't think
It doesn't exist
If I don't see
It isn't there
If I hide
It won't find me
If I ignore
It won't affect me
If I don't believe
It isn't true
If I don't except
It doesn't happen
If I don't grieve
It will be fine
If I don't do anything
Then anything can't happen.

**Neil Thornton  (15)**
**Corfe Hills School**

# Idols

No one beats my idol,
She goes by the name of Aretha,
Although my friends say that she's well bad,
I swear they've never seen her.

I couldn't believe when it came to me,
That she is frightened of the stage,
But I make no mistake, her voice really is great,
As she sings the notes on every page.

Stevie Wonder is another I admire,
For his work on those ivory keys,
He plays bass guitar, drums, and harmonica too,
Even though his eyes never see.

His suspended 4ths, dom, 7ths and major 7ths,
Are some of the chords he uses,
When I try to play 'I Wish'
Those chords are really confusing.

Last but not least is Chaka Khan,
Whose real name is Yvette Stevens
And whoever thinks they can match her voice,
I'll tell you that stuff is for dreamers.

Her talent was soon recognised,
When she was a very young child,
She started a band when she was 15
And man, her hair was wild!

As you can see I have only chosen three,
But I'm telling you, there is loads more,
Like Jools Holland, Marvin Gaye, Earth, Wind and Fire
And I give them each a high score.

They're the ones who inspire to sing and to play,
On my instruments each and every day,
One day I hope to look through their eyes
And see everything their way.

**Emily Francis  (13)**
**Corfe Hills School**

# Dancing!

I like to skip and sing and prance,
But most of all I love to dance!
I go after school on Monday,
To dance all the hours away!
A whole lesson of tap, tap, tap,
We all deserve a great big clap!
Also the warm-ups and disco,
For all of us it's go, go, go!
And with our lessons in ballet,
There is no time for us to play!
Once a year we perform a show,
When all our talent is to glow!
Twice a year we do our exams,
All nervous but happy as lambs!
Although the dancing year is done,
We will be back to have more fun!

**Ellena Kapoor  (13)**
**Corfe Hills School**

# The Creature

The creature
Was as round as the moon
Six eyes he had
And his teeth looked like doom
His hair was brown
And his knees were green
He was the most ugliest thing I'd ever seen
As he came to the entrance
Of his strange UFO
He looked at me
And said, 'Hello!'

**Carl Kill  (13)**
**Corfe Hills School**

# The Life From My Soul

The thought of life without you,
Is like the storm overcoming the sun,
The sky caving in on its minute crevices
And the moon and stars coming undone,
Releasing themselves among all life's creations
And maliciously sucking the life from my soul.

For others water creeps from the imaginary images,
Images which view the memories,
Now becoming elusive in their mind,
Creating sorrow deep within their heart and determining pain forever,
Gradually to fade through time.

Now you must understand,
That without you,
My life would be filled with permanent remorse,
For the times we did not share.

**Teshany Perrett-Conn  (13)**
**Corfe Hills School**


# Night-Time Valley

The river cuts its way through the valley,
Like a shining silver ribbon.
As the moon glows down,
Showing the gleaming backs of fish.

The only sound is the leaves rustling,
Any other noise would echo around the hills.
An otter whips into the river from the bank,
Its smooth, sleek swimming barely makes a ripple.

When dawn breaks light seeps over the hills
And the golden morning sun shines in my eyes.
Out come the early wakers and with them the noise,
Peaceful night-time must wait the day to come again.

**David Charlston  (14)**
**Corfe Hills School**

# War

Our troops are marching forward
Some will bite the dust
Will they survive this battle?
For their country's sake, they must.

The enemy is visible
Their planes fly overhead
Machine gunfire on our frontline
200 men lay dead

We then return the fire
With our heavy tanks
There is much death in the enemy fleet
There's panic within the ranks

Now both armies charge forward
Firing as they go
Dreading, fearing that later on
Their blood will stain the snow

There is but one survivor
Our head sergeant alone
So go and send the chopper out
1 trooper's coming home

The result of this battle
Many widowed wives
For in this battle all their husbands
Sadly lost their lives

So conflict is just foolish
And I wish war would cease
For all that this amazing world needs
Is everlasting peace.

**Aaron Revel (13)**
**Corfe Hills School**

# Happy Birthday, Mum

Happy birthday, Mum, I'm sending you one request,
'Cause you really are number one, you truly are the best,
My one request to you is to always be there for me,
Far into the future for as long as I can see,
You'll always rise above the other parents that you know,
You don't have a schedule, you just go with the flow,
If we were ever parted, I would surely have to die,
I could never live without you, if I had to, I would cry,
When I grow up, I want to have the same point of view,
Have the confidence that you have and do just what you do,
You've taught me obvious things that stare me in the face,
Thanks to you my walk of life will never be a race,
You've always been there for me through the good times and the bad,
You protect me when I'm hurting and cheer me up when I'm sad,
You're my biggest inspiration, what I am is down to you,
Whatever we've been faced with, we've always pulled right through,
People say we're similar, we look and act the same,
So when I get in trouble, I know exactly who to blame,
You set a good example, I know who to follow,
Speak my mind all of the time and in self-pity never wallow,
I never want to betray the trust you're always giving,
I'll look back and know from you what's an honest living,
As long as you're backed up, you never can go wrong,
Writing down your good points would just take too long,
So this is my effort to prove how special you are,
To prove that you are unique and together we'll go far,
So keep my little poem to you and cherish it forever more,
'Cause life's a never-ending journey, never slam the door!

**Rochelle Drew  (15)**
**Corfe Hills School**

# When I Was Young

That time of year had come round again,
Time to see Santa in his den.

On Christmas Eve late at night,
I saw such a beautiful, wonderful sight.

Eight reindeer, a sleigh and Santa too,
Coming around with presents for you.

Wearing my pyjamas, I wanted to explore,
Could it be real? I went to see more.

I saw him again as he turned to go home,
He shot out of sight, I stood like a gnome.

I went back inside and crept into bed,
The thought of no presents were filling my head.

I closed my eyes and dropped off to sleep,
I woke up next morning, but I did not weep.

I saw all my presents and opened them up,
Three games, a book, a toy car and a truck.

I played with my toys, all through the day,
Until it was time to put them away.

**Christopher Danvers  (13)**
**Corfe Hills School**

# Queen Elizabeth II

The Queen has been on the throne for over 50 years,
Living through triumphs and many, many tears,
At the age of 77 she is still reigning strong,
But how long will it be before Prince Charles comes along?

No matter what people say,
She rules the country her own way,
Sometimes she wears her sparkling crown,
Without a trace of a single frown.

1977 was the year of her Silver Jubilee,
It was celebrated in England and made her full of glee,
She has been on the throne since June '53
And has proved to many she is the best queen she can be.

Prince Charles is the next in line
And often has friends round to dine,
Princess Diana was his wife,
But sadly an accident ended her young life!

The Queen has been on the throne for over 50 years,
Living through triumphs and many, many tears,
At the age of 77 she is still reigning strong,
But how long will it before Prince Charles comes along?

**Laura Birch  (13)**
**Corfe Hills School**

# Books

Some big, some small,
Some short, some tall,
Some fat, some thin,
With pictures in.

Romance, action, horror too,
Maybe even a thriller or two,
Animals, action and sci-fi,
Not take your fancy, I ask you why?
How about family, fantasy or sport,
Do you want a second thought?
How about classics, suspense or non-fiction,
There's plenty for you to choose from.

So, whether it's big or small,
Short or tall,
Fat, thin
Or with pictures in,
*Read it!*

**Loren Dowding (13)**
**Corfe Hills School**

# Love

She sits beside her lover,
Beneath the old oak tree,
Initials carved into the bark,
They last eternally.

**Anna Tabrah (13)**
**Corfe Hills School**

# Forgotten

Where's the car?
Should I wait?
Am I too far?
Oh how I hate
To be forgotten

What's the time?
Where is everyone?
It's a crime
They must have gone
And I've been forgotten

Back to the school
To ask for a phone
There should be a rule
That no mums go home
And leave their child forgotten.

**Naomi Pearce  (13)**
**Corfe Hills School**


# Forgotten?

You are black;
You are forgotten.

Application for asylum is rebuked,
Famine and death are 'not reasons'.

You are enshrouded in the mass of mankind,
All oblivious of your mere existence.

Your appearance is different, your skin is too,
But your soul remains intact.

You have no possessions, no food, no water,
Only relations, loyalty and individuality.

You are black;
You are forgotten.

**David Hoyland  (13)**
**Corfe Hills School**

# My Turn!

Shaking like a feather,
I am a nervous wreck,
About to go on stage,
Is it my turn yet?

Cheering, raving crowds,
Applauding for the others,
They have all done so well,
Proud, they have made their mothers.

I am running through my lines,
Frustrated, I cannot recall,
What do I say?
My mind has forgotten all.

I get in the queue,
The clapping audience I hear,
As the curtains go up,
I fill up with fear.

Rows and rows of people,
Are staring up at me,
I open my mouth,
But the words in my mind,
I cannot see.

Blinded by the lights,
I look to the ground,
Suddenly they come to me,
My words, I have found.

I open my mouth,
I speak my part
And the joy of happiness,
Then reaches my heart.

**Kimberley Inman (14)**
**Corfe Hills School**

# These Four Walls

Here I am, all alone,
Sitting in this prison cell,
These four walls that keep me in,
Trap me in this living Hell.

I'm scared my sanity is going,
I can't think straight anymore,
Torn from my family for two long years,
Due to this evil war.

My cell is damp and dark,
With no hint of light,
No sense of what is around me,
How can this be right?

I've had no food for several days,
My stomach cries to be fed,
My body is now limp and weak,
It's no use; all hope has fled.

Starved of food, love and company.
Loneliness is what I fear,
No one to share my inner thoughts,
No one who would want to hear.

Tears like blood from my wounded soul,
Slowly roll down my face,
How could I be forgotten, here,
In this dreadful, miserable place?

The only way I will keep sane,
Is to forget about the past,
This war will end in the future,
I only hope my sanity will last . . .

**Rebecca Clarke  (13)**
**Corfe Hills School**

# Ti-co

Ti-co was my pony
And
Ti-co was my friend

She made me feel
So happy
From the love that she
Would send

I'd give her hugs
And kisses
Her blaze was as
White as snow

Whenever she was sad
She would tell you
You would know

So now I have to
Leave her
My heart was
Broken so

She will always be
With me
She will never, ever go.

**Sarah Froud  (12)**
**Cranborne County Middle School**


# Test

Now I lay me down to rest,
I pray I pass tomorrow's test,
If I should die before I wake,
That's one less test I have to take!

**Annaliese Allcock  (11)**
**Cranborne County Middle School**

# No One Was There

She walked around the earthly place,
But not one expression came to her face,
She walks round where no blackbirds sing,
She thought she was controlled by puppet strings.

She searched around for life out there,
But nothing, nothing made her stare,
I wonder why she was so still,
Standing from the top of the hill.

She stumbles down almost to fall,
How could that be, that hill so tall,
She stood upright, then looks again,
She peers around for women or men.

Nobody came, it was her alone,
She starts to cry and whine and moan,
She wonders why nobody came,
Nobody did, what a shame.

She starts to look for something new,
She looks in the sky but no birds flew,
So she looked ahead, but nothing was there,
There could be a reason but obviously they didn't care.

**Ellie Killeen  (11)**
**Cranborne County Middle School**


# You've Tied The Knot At Last!

Hurray, hurray, you're there at last,
You've tied the knot and are ready to blast,
You're good together, you're great together,
You fit together so perfectly,
If you're ever apart, you'll be lost,
You couldn't live without each other,
Now you've tied the knot.

**Laura House  (11)**
**Cranborne County Middle School**

# Love

Love can be as sweet as curry
And as hot as a chilli pepper

Love can be like a smooth bit of silk
Laying on your bed

Love is out there everyone
Even those that don't have love yet

Love can be as solid as steel
A bit of iron that should not break

Love is here, love is there
Love is everywhere

Love can be different
Love can be Eros, Storage
Phios and there is Agapay
Agapay is the most important
Because Agapay means that you love your family.

**Clayton Godfrey**
**Cranborne County Middle School**


# Bullying

It's not very nice to be bullied,
You're kicked,
Called names,
Hit all over again,
It's not at all nice to be bullied,
Why me?
You ask,
While you're being kicked,
I know this 'cause it's happened -
Happened to me.

**Katie Kynaston  (11)**
**Cranborne County Middle School**

# Gone

Playing in the garden on a sunny day,
We thought he'd gone to get the ball
But he'd ran away.

We thought he would come back soon,
But eleven days went by,
We searched high and low,
Just to hear him cry.

Every field and wood,
We searched every day and night,
Shouting, calling, yelling his name,
Not a sound in sight.

One day after school,
We received a phone call,
It was the RSPCA,
They said they found a black Labrador,
We went to see it right away.

It wasn't ours, it was too plump,
They said they found it tied to a wooden stump.
The next day I went to school,
Wishing for the right phone call.

When I got home,
My mum said there was a surprise,
I went in the kitchen and saw two sad-looking eyes,
It was Tom, our dog,
I was so happy and so glad,
Now I know I am so lucky,
I will never be sad.

**Sophie Court (12)**
**Cranborne County Middle School**

## Sudden Death

Day dew droplets fall upon the meadow
As the buttercups sway in the breeze
Life is new and fresh and life is good
As the ball of fire shines through the trees
The dew dries off and life turns dry
And everything becomes a big fat lie
Illness comes as sadness arrives
I then find out life has died.

**Libby Bell  (11)**
Cranborne County Middle School


## Twin Towers Ballad

One day there were two towers
They were up high in the sky
They were up there for hours and hours
But one day everything must die

Two planes, two towers
Upon the clouds
For hours and hours
Standing so proud

The plane flew past
And turned around
And at last they crashed
But the towers fell to the ground

The towers so tall
But fell to the ground
And became so small
As people gathered round

People died
In the awesome fall
Families cried
Their tears made a waterfall.

**Matthew Macdonald  (12)**
Oakmead College of Technology

# My Own Ballad On My Dog

Once she was a puppy
Jumping around and around
Barking all the time
Flinging from the ground

Now she's older she becomes more hyper
Her name is Penny
She is now four
We would not choose the name Lenny

Cuddly and cute
So fun to be with and to play
Runs really fast
Nearly the end of the day

Her newly white coat
Her big beady eyes
Her little wagging tail
Around her neck her little ties

Her big wide mouth
Her little ears so, so sweet
Her little feet so cute
She loves her meat.

**Lauren Clark  (12)**
**Oakmead College of Technology**

# Love Poem

Roses are red
Violets are blue
I am thinking of you
I love you
And when you are away
I am missin' you
Cos I love you.

**Mack Bishop  (11)**
**Oakmead College of Technology**

# Jessica And Holly

There were two little girls
Called Jessica and Holly,
They were always together,
Laughing and jolly.

They were always out playing,
In sun, rain or snow,
Always something to do,
Always somewhere to go.

It was one day,
When they went out to play,
They were out a long time,
Had they forgotten the way?

It became 9 o'clock,
There was still no sign
Of the two little girls,
Who stepped over the line.

The police were called,
But still nothing found,
They couldn't of vanished into
Thin air.

Suspects were found
All over the town,
Police were still looking
Around and around.

Days went by,
Eventually they were found,
Both together,
Laid under the ground.

Families were upset
At the sight
Of the two dead children,
Who should have been alright.

**Courtney Esson (12)**
**Oakmead College of Technology**

# A Ballad Of My Cousin, Ayla

We didn't know why,
But she did it sometimes.
She'd skip in the front garden,
As it isn't a crime.

She'd skip and sing,
Like nothing had gone wrong.
As she started on the pavement,
We noticed she'd been out there too long.

So we went to collect her
And she was lying on a bar.
It was horrible, the sight,
There was blood on a stranger's car.

In hospital we ran up to her
And hoped she was OK,
But as the paramedics just said,
'Please leave her to lay.'

They came to take her,
To take her away.
We didn't understand,
That that was her last day.

So everyone was quiet,
At the funeral with a tear.
For every single song
That Ayla could not hear.

We had her cremated,
We thought it be best.
Then little children
Couldn't be naughty pests.

We knew she liked the water,
So we let her be free.
As we stand on a cliff,
We sprinkled her ashes into the sea . . .

**Charmaine Slaughter  (12)**
**Oakmead College of Technology**

# Mum

*(Dedicated to a dear mum, Julie Nash)*

A complete family, they had all said
When we were born to Mum and Dad
One boy, one girl, twins they'd had
A bright happy future for us lay ahead

But six months later came the fateful day
While driving down the motorway
Out of the blue came a terrible crash
Caused by someone who liked to dash

Dad, brother and me just walked away
But with us no more would Mum play
No more would we wake up to her smiling face
As Dad tried his best to take her place

Now twelve years later, I still wonder why
She was the one who had to die
Why she was the one taken away that day
To break up the complete happy family?

**Hayley Goddard  (12)**
**Oakmead College of Technology**


# Football

Football, football everywhere
Football fly here and there
You feel good when the football goes up, up and away
Into the back of the net for a win today

You grab the ball and go running around the pitch
Passing and shouting, ignoring your stitch

You hear the full-time whistle
You won one-nil
You kept a clean sheet
And we're going to win again next week.

**Sam Reagen  (12)**
**Oakmead College of Technology**

# Sam Barnes

He always loved his sport
Like football and swimming
He never failed to help
Because he was always willing

He was always a happy boy
He always had a smile
He also liked cross-country
And also ran that extra mile

It all happened so quickly
It was like a flash
We all stopped and stared
Then we all ran in a dash

He was rushed into hospital
And had lots of tests
They found a brain tumour
And then he had to have lots of rest

It went on for a year
He struggled for a long time
He was bored in his bed
So he tried to write a rhyme

It all ended so quickly
Now we are raising money
And we are doing a sponsored walk
And he was funny.

**Jack Holmes (12)**
**Oakmead College of Technology**

# Dreaming

Here I am sitting at home all alone,
Dreaming of fantasies in a world of my own;
In my house without my friends, just me,
While the rain pours down, my mind runs free.

In my world the summer's the hottest around,
In the autumn a layer of red leaves cover the ground.
My trees are chocolate with leaves of jelly,
This is much better than watching the telly!

My mountains are ice cream with a cherry on their tops,
You see where the sky begins and the land stops.
My bed is a four-poster, fancy and tall
And thousands of colours cover my walls.

Here the water slides look great fun
And I'll sit on the beaches under the sun.
In the night, I'll visit the spas,
In the finest hotels I'll meet all the stars.

Here the books and stories are anything but a bore,
I've got so many books, but I'll have some more.
There is a huge spread of colour all around,
It's amazing what can be found.

These are just memories, memories of mine,
But I can look back on them, so that's fine.
There are so many places to go and see,
But nothing compares to my fun fantasy.

**Hannah Boyce  (13)**
**Oakmead College of Technology**

# Two Sweet Girls

There were two young girls called Holly and Jessica,
They were best friends,
They had been for seven years,
Who was the one that had to press send?

They went out to town,
On one sunny day,
Never returned again,
Had they forgotten the way?

When they didn't return
At 7 o'clock,
Their mums called the police,
Who looked at the dock.

The police looked and looked,
But still no sign,
Months had went,
Who was the person who stepped over the line?

The mums were worried,
The police carried a load,
Until they were found,
Right by a road.

When the police told the mums,
They were terribly upset,
The two girls were dead,
Was this a bet?

**Siobhan Hiscock (12)**
**Oakmead College of Technology**

# Holly And Jessica

Holly and Jessica
One day vanished
From their homes
Were they banished?

They were gone
But who had seen
The tracks
Where the girls had been?

When they left
Not a squeak
No door, window open
Not even a creak

Last seen in a car park
Searched for high and low
By friends and family
And people they know

We wish one day
They will be found
Until that day
We hear not a sound

If they were taken away
Till this day
Holly and Jessica
Will they find their way?

**Sophie Lawrence  (13)**
**Oakmead College of Technology**

# They Were Once Standing

They were the tallest buildings ever,
The Twin Towers stood up together
And everyone hoped
They would be there forever.

It was a fine day on September 11th,
When a plane came in, the ground started to quiver,
But no one knew the disaster would happen,
When the two towers started to shiver.

The plane came in
And *bang*, it had landed
Into one of the towers
That was standing.

Half an hour has passed
And another plane came,
It started to circle the towers
But then came back again.

The plane came closer
And *bang*, it landed,
Into the other tower
That was standing.

People jumping from the buildings,
As the towers came down and landed
On the ground covered in dust and people
And that was the end of the Twin Towers that was once standing!

**Sherry Lumber  (12)**
**Oakmead College of Technology**

# My Ballad On Sarah Payne

Sarah was a lovely girl
And what happened, happened so fast
She was just playing in a field
Which was very vast

She didn't return for dinner
Her grandma was really scared
They looked for her everywhere
I wonder if she was dared?

Days passed and weeks passed
But where could she of gone?
She couldn't of gone very far
Oh I wonder what she's done?

Months passed slowly
The police were involved
They said to put her on the news
So the press got involved

Sarah was found
Lying on the ground
She had been murdered
And everyone frowned

Sarah's family were angry
With the person that had done the crime
Who had taken Sarah away forever
Oh I do hope her killer is fined

Sarah was buried
But no one will forget
How she died so tragically
I know I won't forget.

**Kristie Henley  (12)**
**Oakmead College of Technology**

# Nature

Trees, fleas
And bumblebees
All are alive
So help them survive
By learning this rhyme
Don't waste paper
Use both sides
That will help save nature
And all its creatures
To stay alive
Don't fish and make my wish come true
Believe me, you will notice it around you
Cats and rats
Dogs and hogs
Chimpanzees and monkeys
They all have homes
Like garden gnomes
That live in the garden behind you
Don't chop down trees, please
Don't sneeze over bees, please
Don't touch a flea's knees, please
Look around you when you are out
Without a doubt you can see
Trees, fleas and bumblebees
Make a chart and write it down
Don't worry if people call you a clown
For writing down
What you can see
All around.

**Helen McCann (11)**
**Oakmead College of Technology**

# My Midsummer Night's Dream

I have done a play
A Midsummer Night's Dream
We got all our actors
And then worked as a team

We sang and danced
And made the audience laugh
We had our costumes
And looked rather daft!

Everybody got their scripts
And learnt them by the next day
We rehearsed our parts
And heard what he had to say

So after school we rehearsed
Until we got it right
Mr Evans would shout
So we wouldn't fight

We got all together
And needed to do it on a stage
We went to the Tivoli Theatre
And it was a massive outrage

It was a Wednesday evening
And all our nerves were shaking
The play went well
And all were baking

The crowd cheered and clapped
We were all filled with happiness and cheer
Hoping to do this again
Then all said, 'Bye,' and, 'see you next year!'

**Melissa Tuck  (12)**
**Oakmead College of Technology**

# Holly And Jessica

Holly and Jessica,
Gone one day,
Never coming home,
Disappeared in May.

Gone a year,
Through the thickened frost,
Mumbling, shaking in fear,
It is like a coin that has been tossed.

All day and night,
Throughout the week,
This is their battle that they have to fight,
All lonely, not a creak.

I do wonder where they are,
Where they've gone
And how far?
Every day the sun shone.

Finding them I'm ever so keen,
Will they be dirty
Or will they be clean?
Will they come back polite and courteous?

As young as young can be,
Will they be found again?
It's like a sting in my knee,
It starts to drizzle, then pours down buckets of rain.

Men in black,
Vanishing less and less,
There used to be a stack,
Take a chance, or take a guess?

Bundles of flowers been placed,
But why?
Water trickles down upon my face,
Why did they die?

**Emma Ross  (12)**
**Oakmead College of Technology**

# The Ballad Of Karen Whistler

Riding in the woods
Trotting by the stream
The horses started galloping
They thought it was a dream

Going back along the river
Everyone was quiet
The ambulance sped by them
Like there'd been a riot

Six days later she woke up
Her husband's heart was light
This is because he said to her
She'd given such a fright

She made it back to England
And shortly she was home
With everybody visiting
She'd never be alone

Though life is not quite normal
I have my mother back
And one thing is for certain
She'll not take another hack.

**Georgina Whistler  (12)**
**Oakmead College of Technology**


# July

The sun shimmers on the sea,
The beach is the place you'll want to be,
Golden sand and deckchairs out,
Hoards of people sitting about,
Children playing in the sand,
With buckets and spades in their hands,
Seaweed, pebbles, crabs and shells,
An ice cream van ringing its bell.

**Carla Fletcher  (12)**
**Oakmead College of Technology**

# Ballad

When Jessica and Holly were gone
We all hoped and prayed
For them to be alive
And put who did this away

When Jessica and Holly went missing
We were hoping they were alive
And not to be in hospital
But home, alive

When the police found something
When they searched a school
It did look good
It did look nice

When the police arrested someone
We wondered who it was
Could it be a man
Or another lass?

Then they found them in a forest
Found them wrapped up in a tent
With no sign of life.

**Kerry Andrews  (12)**
**Oakmead College of Technology**


# Animals

Animals are fluff balls,
They really are cute,
A hamster, rabbit, guinea pig, dog and cats too,
I have a hamster of my own,
She is a real small thing,
Her name is Millie.
I do like other animals but I have one already,
If you do have one, then look after it, really do,
It does not matter what colour they are,
Just love them as much as you can.

**Natasha Cruickshank  (11)**
**Oakmead College of Technology**

# My Pet Rabbit

Rabbits are friendly,
Rabbits are sweet.
They're lots of fun
And have small feet!

They love to skip,
They love to run,
They have lots of cuddles
And fabulous fun!

Some are brown,
Some are white,
They have lots of teeth,
But they never bite!

The best thing I like about them,
Is their fluffy tail,
Not forgetting the little pink tongue,
When they are for sale!

Mine's called Missy,
What's yours called?
She is a beige colour,
But is never fooled!

Rabbits need lots of love
And looking after,
They're never any trouble
And give you lots of fun!

**Charlotte Millett  (12)**
**Oakmead College of Technology**

# A Ballad Of James Bulger

A boy named James Bulger
He was only two years of age
Shopping with his mummy
Taken from her in rage

The two boys who took him
Horrible ones they were
They tied him to a railway track
And his life was over

Another innocent child
Lying there in pain
Crying for his mummy
And then went the train

He never went to school
Or had a wife
He never had any children
He didn't have a life

We know he went to Heaven
He didn't do anything wrong
The boys went to prison
But not for very long

They got new identities
Moved to a different place
No one knows where they are
Because there's no trace.

**Sian-Louise Morgan  (12)**
**Oakmead College of Technology**

# Bullying!

It's not fair being picked on,
I've been trying to fit in for so long!
I try to act like the other kids,
But they still think I am weird!

They throw things at me in class time
And hit me three times a day
And at playtime I sit and repeatedly say
'Will you be my friend, please?
Who I can rely on every day!'
But they all just ignore me
And pretend I'm not there!

So I've written this poem
Just for you, just to see
I need a friend, a caring friend
Who thinks of me as me!

**Emma Wall  (11)**
**Oakmead College of Technology**


# Siege

As the war rages on,
By the good castle, Saelon,
The dragons take flight,
As the soldiers prove their might,
Surrounded by rivers of blood.

Dragon's claws smash
And knight's swords clash,
As man and beast's own kin,
Wonder who will lose  and who will win?

Both lie down upon the moor,
Still and quiet for evermore.

**Robyn Frost  (11)**
**Oakmead College of Technology**

# Bullying

At my school there are lots of bullies
But I'm not one of them
I always get bullied, but the teacher never listens
And they always get away with it

At playtime I have to lock myself in the toilet
Because I am way too scared
I have no friends that never help
Maybe it's because I wear glasses

Maybe it's because I'm not as pretty as the other girls?
I don't know but I'm a big misfit
Why is it always me?
When I walk past someone, I end up on the floor

What is the matter with me?
Why is it always me?
Someone help me
Is there anyone out there that is like me?

If there is, then someone please
Please, please be my friend
Because nobody will
Come and help me!

**Zoe Conway (11)**
**Oakmead College of Technology**

# I Have Done It!

I cannot wait
It's in two weeks
I am going to the world's
It's like having treats

Yes, I've got my kit
It's the colour of the flag
Red, white and blue
Shame we did not get a free bag

Something has come true
Something I have dreamed
I'm going to Germany
When I found out, I screamed

I am going with my best friend
We are doing this for fun
We are pleased that we go there
We are coming down on you like a tonne

Better watch out
We are coming for you
We have been practising it
So watch out for us two.

**Katy Janson  (12)**
**Oakmead College of Technology**

# Sports!

There are loads of different sports,
Football, rugby, netball and many, many more,
Some are fun and some are boring,
They are all very energetic.

Dance is my favourite sport,
It's so much fun to do,
I could dance all day long,
Dance makes me smile,
I love it when I get to dance,
It's boring when there's nothing to do.

My friends like swimming and karate,
They say it's fun to do,
They're energetic and I really think it's true,
I would never disagree with them,
For they're always right.

**Kirsty Rickman  (11)**
**Oakmead College of Technology**

# Untitled

To see life as a flower
So you can plant it
Water it, give light and love
See the colourful petals
Representing a hint of the beauty
Of Mother Nature
As the seasons change
So do the flowers
Not so bright and colourful
The damp and cold set in
So why not try and see life
As a flower?

**John Elliott  (12)**
**Oakmead College of Technology**

# My Best Friend

Shannon is my best friend because
She talks to me when I'm sad
When I go on my skateboard she does too
I hope that she doesn't turn bad

When we grow up she will come shopping
For some chains for our jeans
And new T-shirts and jeans and shoes and more
When we go shopping we will be in our teens

Mine and Shannon's favourite band is Busted
We are crazy, if a limo comes past you will hear a scream
We think Busted are in it and they have come to pick us up
Me, Shannon and Jade are one hell of a team

Shannon has a brother and a sister
I have one brother nicknamed the 'Sado'
Shannon's brother is called Jordan
And his nickname is definitely the 'Bado'.

**Emma Gill  (12)**
**Oakmead College of Technology**


# Bullying

I don't like school that much nowadays
It's just not fun anymore
I go to Oakmead College and we have more lessons than four
Every day when I wake up, I dread going to school
There are people there who think they are really cool
They really don't care about my feelings because
They are always picking on me
But one day I will go up to them and say
'Why are you bullying me?'
I just want to have some peace and be by my own
Because I don't have any friends and I am all alone.

**Sam Greer  (11)**
**Oakmead College of Technology**

# A Rad Sports Poem

There was a school like Oakmead
We couldn't stop going in the lead
There are a wide variety of sports
They even had tennis courts
Volleyball, basketball, netball too
Each of these is very new

Achievements, awards, prizes too
You'll like one, I guarantee you
For rugby you need the right kit
You also need to be very fit
These new sports are very lush
Each of these you do in a rush.

**Tyler Molyneaux  (12)**
**Oakmead College of Technology**


# How Are You?

Hello there,
I haven't spoken to you for ages, how are you?
Just come back from holiday, had lots of things to do.
The weather was great, the beach and the hotel too.
There were plenty of markets, a lot of places to buy food,
My French was a bit rusty but most people were friendly.
We had our car, so we could visit places easily,
The weather was hot most of the time we were there,
But the sea was refreshing, so I didn't really care.
We got plenty of exercise, due to our bikes,
Dad went out for his early morning hikes.
Anyway enough about me, we could meet up,
(Something to do),
I haven't spoken to you for ages, so how are you?

**Charlotte Ingham  (13)**
**Parkstone Grammar School**

# Dreams

There he is . . .
I can't believe he's looking at me.
Wait, is he looking at me?
At me?
No, he can't be.
Why would he be looking at me?
Me? I mean come on . . .
Ooh, he's coming over.
Over here!
Is this happening?
Me? He can't be.
There's no one behind me . . .
He must be
Nah, he wouldn't.
He's here!
Oh my god . . .
He's so gorgeous.
Everything about him.
Just as I imagined.
He's talking to me!
*To me!*
Oh my god.
This must be a dream.
But every word, every touch . . .
It all seems so real.
Why would he be talking to me?
He's just as I imagined,
Tall, beautiful brown eyes,
This can't be happening.
This has to be the best day of my life.
Wait, he's leaning forward . . .
*He's kissing me!*
The way his hands touch my back . . .
Oh my god!

How can this be happening
To me?
*Brrrr*
'Wake up honey,
Time for school.'

**Lara Bunter  (14)**
**Parkstone Grammar School**


# The Closing Of The Day

In the closing of the day,
the elderly giant stands alone.
Her branches swaying in the wind,
each a special child of hers.
Small and thin, large and tall,
but others cannot be seen at all.

Alone she stands awaiting spring,
where her youth's beauty will blossom.
Her leaves shall shine like the wind,
whereas now they float to the ground
like a raindrop falling from the sky.

Life is breaking as she waits,
for the sunset to go down,
so she can rest in peace,
but still she lingers,
in the glow of the dangerous sunset,
for her autumn misery to end.

**Lizzie Porter  (12)**
**Parkstone Grammar School**

# To Autumn

The mist hangs down in sombre veil,
In mourning of the coming hail,
An impenetrable haze of white.
A thick, loose grip around the eyes,
A soothing cover for forgotten skies,
But filtered with a rosy light.
Behind the mist spreads icy blue,
Clear and crisp and chilly too,
With no cloud to be seen.
The now tamed light of flaming sun,
A golden smudge; the only one,
Gazes down on glistening green.
Crystallised, the tiny blades,
Of lush green grass, ten thousand shades,
They gaze in awe at the above.
Wear dewdrop medals in their pride,
Like tiny soldiers, side by side,
Nature's hand in greener glove.
Flowers shrink to deeper sleep,
The drizzle falls as the skies weep
And foxes curl up underground.
Men remain in tall brick huts,
While squirrels hunt for fruit and nuts,
While mist muffles the sound.
Frosty coat on window glass,
Cars beep with anger as they pass,
The tar mark under slippery sheen.
People pull their coats about,
In weaving crowds, in and out,
As everything does gleam.
Car bonnets frown at coming cold,
An ominous wrath to behold,
They grumble and they moan.
The breath of people melt to frost,
They hang their heads at summer's lost,
As howling winds do groan.

Leaves are swirling in the breeze,
A confetti gift from dozing trees,
Red, amber, orange, gold
And the world awaits the winter white,
Of glittering snow in pink gold light,
A promise future holds.

**Marienna Pope-Weidemann  (12)**
**Parkstone Grammar School**


# Ocean

As the warm sun rises,
In the misty horizon behind their ship.
It moves swiftly onwards,
Gliding silently across the delicate sea.
Orange, yellow and red looming above.
While in a sheet of blue below,
The creatures of the deep swim freely.
It's like a vibrant dream,
Full of intimidating sights and romantic scenery.
Warm graceful, relaxing days,
But it can be a cold, treacherous, dramatic nights.
The sea is like a sink with no plug,
A forever flowing tap.
The water ripples as the ship breaks its way through,
Drifting over a carpet of greeny blue.
Towards a freedom of peace and calm,
Inviting them further out.
They glide, a mixture of colours,
Illuminating the way.

**Chloé James  (12)**
**Parkstone Grammar School**

# Anger

I can see him,
Standing before me,
Reaching out as I hold open the door,
A glass of water in one hand,
What do I do?
He's coming towards me,
Closer
And closer.
I'm scared.
My hand slips from the door,
It bangs.
I throw my glass at him,
I missed,
It smashes.
He still proceeds towards the closed door,
I head in the opposite direction,
Past the trophy cabinet.
He doesn't notice,
He opens the oak door
And walks out.
I follow him.

**Mel Moore  (13)**
**Parkstone Grammar School**


# My Bed

I am warm, cosy and inviting,
    Go to sleep,
I will wrap you up till morning's here,
    Don't wake up,
Stay with me until you feel awake,
    I am your friend,
Please stay and keep me company,
    I am your bed,
I hate it when you leave me here,
    I am alone.

**Laura Singleton  (14)**
**Parkstone Grammar School**

# Emotions

What is jealousy?
Jealousy is a wall.
What is a wall?
A wall is anger.
What is anger?
Anger is rejection.
What is rejection?
Rejection is sadness.
What is sadness?
Sadness is fear.
What is fear?
Fear is want.
What is want?
Want is love.
What is love?
Love is jealousy.
What is jealousy?

**Louise Croft (14)**
**Parkstone Grammar School**

# Paradise

Dear Mum . . .
I went to paradise today
It was beautiful
Miles of exotic flowers and hours of sunshine
Silk waters and golden beaches

All my desires and virtues coming true
No more destruction or eyesores
All the family talking to each other again
With no awkward silences
What more could I ask for?

Paradise!

**Rachel Dickenson (13)**
**Parkstone Grammar School**

# Autumn

The season of the fallen leaves,
Hiding the masters of dismount,
Conspiring to allure the unsuspected victim from their steeds,
To an unscheduled meeting with churned, dampened soil
of the woodland floor.
The bell sounds its hypnotic message,
Of leave from battle with autumnal sod and nature's debris.
The warm hut of rest welcomes every inch of battered and torn sinew
And affords glory and adulation for the few.
But the abstract magical sense of adrenalin charged
achievement for the remainder.
After a hard morning in the forest,
O, the wickedness of autumn,
The stench of the place,
With the mud, the blood, the medication and perspiration,
Aspiring from the mound of deserted garments now
Fills the confines for the journey home along wet,
Slippery roads littered with autumn spoils.
But was the toil and graft in vain?

**Emily Hardwicke  (12)**
**Parkstone Grammar School**


# What Will Happen Now? Haiku

The sky is falling,
The world is getting darker,
What will happen now?

**Alice Haw  (13)**
**Parkstone Grammar School**

# Winter

Stealthily creeps in,
Whilst all are turned away,
Unnoticed,
Silently,
Snatches away all warmth
And hope,
Showing no signs of mercy,
As it comes upon shivering animals,
Whilst wrapping itself,
And the world,
In a coal-like,
Black,
Blanket of darkness,
Sunless,
Sombre,
Cheerless,
Chill,
Winter . . .

**Amanda Callaghan  (13)**
**Parkstone Grammar School**


# Sadness

If sadness controlled your life,
What would you do?
It feels bigger than you
And yet it is
It's always there
At the back of your mind
From then it slowly declines
Consumes you
To the very last piece
It holds your heart
And your soul
Leaving you in pain.

**Dom Marriott  (13)**
**Parkstone Grammar School**

# Mirror

Mirror, mirror on the wall,
Who's the fairest of them all?
Am I the ugliest thing you've seen,
Or am I good-looking, a beauty queen?

Why do you mimic the things I do,
Are you a shadow, are you true?
Do you lie about the way I look?
You seem to read me like a book.

Do you see me the way others do,
Or am I just another image to you?
Tell me the truth because I'm unsure,
Will you remember me for evermore?

Do you get bored of sitting there alone?
Do you get bored of hearing people moan?
Mirror, mirror on the wall,
Who's the fairest of them all?

**Emily Watson  (13)**
**Parkstone Grammar School**


# Silence

Silence before the storm
Is what they always say.
Electric white,
Thunder and crash rend the air,
Then silence,
Always silence,
The sky, purple with anger,
The townshadows in fear.
Another boom from the bleak heavens,
But, as they always say,
There's silence before the storm.

**Laura Cake  (12)**
**Parkstone Gramma School**

# Death At My Door

He's watching me
Waiting so patiently
At my door
He's watching
And waiting for me

I feel he is closer
He tapped his knuckles on my door
I saw his face through the window
He's still waiting and watching for me

He's clever now
I saw his bright red eyes
Shining in the dark
I heard his breath
His harsh, shallow breathing

I saw his cloak
I heard his step upon the stair
I saw the handle turn
As he entered the room
The darkness spread

He doesn't wait anymore
No longer is he at my door
He carried me to my eternal rest
He told me it was for the best.

**Christina Badger  (13)**
**Parkstone Grammar School**

# Friendship

I know you are going to be there until the very end
Because you are not just my soulmate, you are my life
                                   and my best friend
And I know you are going to be there whichever way we bend
But whatever happens to both of us, my love I will always send

If I do not see you for a few hours or a little while
I just sit and think of your face and it always brings a smile
If I have a problem I know which number I have to dial
For you I would run the marathon and I can't even run a mile

I love the way you care about me and the way you sit and stare
Because finding somebody like you is very, very rare
Nobody ever sees us as two people we are a pair
And everything I do, I do it because I care

Just really want you to know I would do absolutely anything for you
Because you really mean the world to me, honestly you do
I have so much admiration for you, so much you don't have a clue
And I also love that feeling that you are always there for me too

You are worth so much more than silver, gold and pearl
You taste nicer than a chocolate bar, Mars bar, Snicker and Twirl
I know it does not matter if my hair is straight or curled
Because to the world you can be one person, but to one
                                   person you can be the world.

**Lauren Howlett  (15)**
**Parkstone Grammar School**

# Love's Young Dream

A woman stands hungry and lonely,
As she cradles her son from the world.
She stares down at him, desperate and thirsty,
As she cradles her son from the world.
A single tear falls down her weary cheek,
As she cradles her son from the world.
His sleeping hand clings to her; she makes no move,
But cradles her son from the world.

She has seen war and disease,
That's why she cradles her son from the world.
She knows life is unfair,
That's why she cradles her son from the world.
She knows his life will be hard,
That's why she cradles her son from the world.
She knows her love will not save him,
That's why she cradles her son from the world.

**Rhiannon Roderick  (12)**
**Parkstone Grammar School**

# Death

He is everywhere
Creeping slowly, silently
Through the black shadows
Watching, waiting for his chance
Until he decides
It is time for you to leave
He struggles with you
He's pulling with all his might
Soon it is over
He defeated you, he won
Now he wants his prize
So he takes the life from you
No one can escape
Eventually you're his . . .

**Emma Tinnion  (13)**
**Parkstone Grammar School**

# The Road To Nowhere

I was there, on that night
In the street,
I stood staring into the face of the moon,
The dark, chill wind
Came whistling around the corner,
I turned,
Looking for something, anything,
A clue to my existence.

Hearing the church bells chime,
I felt a distant comfort covering my heart,
Ding-dong, ding-dong . . .
I strode in time to the chimes,
Heading nowhere, but somewhere,
The curiosity cat inside me, taking over my mind,
I searched the dilapidated surroundings,
For shadows,
But no movement, did I find.

Darkness was upon the town,
Grasping the buildings with its claws,
I felt a sudden shrill of cold,
Moving my spine,
The movement of my legs kept me going,
I stumbled on a cobblestone,
Just as the church bells stopped.

I stopped,
Just standing there,
In that particular street,
I had made it.

I was there; but where?

**Rebecca Hunt (13)**
**Parkstone Grammar School**

# The Tree Of Life

Autumn is here now,
Blustery winds,
Getting colder,
The woods become darker.
The pure green leaves on the trees are turning now,
Into colours of red, orange, yellow and brown.
A great old tree stands isolated in the woods,
Dusty, worn, brown,
Its branches are wide and full of aging leaves.
Each branch reaches out,
As though each are wanting something more from the world
                                        than just life.
The branches represent paths of decision making for the future,
Good or bad,
The choices are hard.
Each aging leaf on the old tree represents your desire to go on,
When you begin to give up, one at a time a leaf will fall, until there
                                        are none left,
To form a path of crispy, crunchy, beautiful colours,
Leading to an unknown world, paradise?
One leaf of orange slowly flutters towards a pond,
The pond is near frozen,
The leaf settles, the corners of the leaf curl inwards,
Shielding itself from the coldness,
Dusk is close at hand, night will soon fall,
But the tree of life is waiting, waiting for someone to go forth
                                        and make life-changing decisions,
Never forget that tree of life,
It's waiting,
Waiting for you.

**Emily Harris (13)**
**Parkstone Grammar School**

# The Ceremony

Mourning tears on a delicate face,
The loss of someone special.
The traditional black,
No blue or white.

The view of her loved one being lowered,
No one there except the lady and the vicar.
Stood in front of the grave,
The stone stating the day of death.

The grave filled up with muddy soil,
A patch of dull brown mud,
The rest all fresh grown grass.
'No!' the lady screams,
As the grave is left deserted.

She is left on her own to sob in the rain,
With no living thing in sight.
No longer can the wind be heard,
Only the crying of the lady.

**Gemma Cargill  (13)**
**Parkstone Grammar School**


# The Mother And Child

A mother is clutching her child,
Protecting her from disease,
Their clothes are dusty like everyone else's
And they're desperate for food.

They have travelled on group journeys,
But they're isolated from the crowd.
She cares for her child,
Love is all they have.

**Anna Stone  (12)**
**Parkstone Grammar School**

# Silver Swan

Sapphire seas shine silently
In sinking sun's shadows
Channel pathed in gold-gilded mystery
Silhouetted over shallow surf swell
Scarcely noticing secret swirl and swish
Of white horses' manes,
Hope sheltered in sun-dappled seawater,
Copper crimson skies, sun shrinking slowly,
Sensational smooth smudge of colour,
Spread strikingly together,
Suddenly sparkling in sea-soothing song,
Stands a ship with silver shimmering sails,
A silver swan gliding gracefully over tranquil satin,
Lulling lonely travellers into secret future,
Soft pearly silver light lapping, luring,
Silky sleek lanterns brightly reflecting lifelong memories,
Time eternally pulling onwards,
Although clouds and storms block success and prosper,
Strive and struggle onwards with stunning strength and determination,
Sea sail swiftly to states of peace,
Dreams, love and soaring success.

**Melissa Elsworth  (12)**
**Parkstone Grammar School**


# Sunlight

Sunlight trickles off his smile
And caresses his soft skin,
It drags its heat across his chest
And rests upon his chin,
It tickles him and when it reaches
His tender heart so bare,
We realise that this thing we've seen,
Is a golden love affair.

**Claire Constantine  (13)**
**Parkstone Grammar School**

# Looking For God

Looking for God
My mind wants to know
My heart wants to find
Where God is living

How do I look?
Where do I look?
High, low, inside or out
Will He be tall or will He be stout?

I looked all night and I looked all day
I looked in the land and by the bay
I looked in the sea and in space
But nothing, nothing, nothing

After my search, I finally found
God, the one, the only one
If you want to look I'll tell you where
Look in yourself and He will be there.

**Nicola Beattie (12)**
**Parkstone Grammar School**

# The Smile

Shining red suit, sparkling pearls,
Elegant as she twists her curls.
Her radiance is not ignored
And many times over it they've roared,
How do you do the subtle thing
That makes us want to dance and sing?
But she never does reply,
Yet she is not something you buy.
Some try to make,
The perfect fake,
But nothing ever could compile,
To the genuine dazzling smile!

**Hazel Wallace (14)**
**Parkstone Grammar School**

# The Unknown

Alien, yet strangely familiar
An undiscovered land that has been seen before
It is hidden, but out in the open for the world to see

Where?

Lonely, yet crowded and popular
An unnamed world with a title
It is a misfit, but also a conformist

Who?

Light, yet dark
Still, but active
Cold, yet warm

How?

Why?

When?

**Charli Watkins (12)**
**Parkstone Grammar School**


# Love Is Like A Butterfly

Love is like a butterfly
It flutters through the air
It surrounds every one of us
And makes us want to care

Its wings so delicate and beautiful
The journey they have to take
It's like a roller coaster ride
But never do they break

No matter what shape and colour
It minds not where it lands
For love is like a butterfly
And both are in God's hands.

**Amy Sparrow (13)**
**Parkstone Grammar School**

# What Is Lightning?

What is lightning?
Is it a tree turned upside-down
Silhouetted in the night sky,
Or the sky cracked open for a split second
Then repaired as quickly as it came?
Could it be a spillage seeping through the sky,
Branching off in all directions,
Thinner and thinner
As it spreads through the starlit sky,
Or it could be God's hand reaching down
Touching the people below him,
His veins turned cold in anger,
Punishing people for their sins.
As I sit at the window,
I wonder all these things,
What is lightning?

**Rosie Browne  (12)**
**Parkstone Grammar School**


# The Storm

The lightning struck the ground,
Leaving a tree in a pile of ashes on the floor,
The powerful electric bolt lit up the whole of the night sky,
Leaving the whole town in danger and terror.

The storm swept through the town with rage and anger,
Setting many objects on fire as it went,
All you could hear was the screams of frightened children,
As the darkness was lit up by a violent flash.

The dramatic bolt, as if the sky was splitting in two,
As the blinding light shone through the night sky,
The deafening thunder left people shocked,
As its fierce sound reached the town.

**Sarah Maiden  (12)**
**Parkstone Grammar School**

# Forlorn Hope

A singular tree in a field of autumn colours,
Old and weathered, awaiting a companion,
Its dominant branches swaying in the breeze,
Whistling a forlorn tune.

The fiery sun beaming down,
Casts a shadow of worry and despair.
There it sinks in its sorrow,
Downwards drowning in the earth below.

Its branches expanding in the merging sky,
Create pathways up in the clouds,
Awaiting the day when someone will come
And join in the journey to friendship.

Until that day the lonely oak stands,
Listening to the conversations around him,
Longing to be part of the fun and laughter,
But too proud to do anything but wait.

**Philippa Rook  (12)**
**Parkstone Grammar School**

# Sleeping Dragon

The vast hillsides are joined like a huge sleeping dragon,
The dragon swallows me up into a great valley
Of trees and trickling streams which creep down
Cracks and dips of its back.

The sheep are like scales on the dragon's spine,
The forest's like sharp claws tucked away under the hills.
The golden sun sets behind the dragon's head
And looks like fire from his mouth.

Smokey clouds rise up from behind his long winding body
Which lies between villages and towns.
He sleeps, never moving, never speaking,
But sleeping and waiting.

**Hannah Elder  (12)**
**Parkstone Grammar School**

# Girl At The Window

Girl at the window,
Devastated, heartbroken, alone.
Nobody understands her,
Her heart, crystal clear, not a drop of guilt,
Innocent . . .
Old, dirty, red sweater,
Wrapped around her,
All she has to keep her warm.
Looking in at the happiness, warmth and enjoyment
Of other children,
Wishing her life was like that.
Her unkempt hair,
Falling onto her shoulders,
Which hold too much already.
All she wishes for,
Is someone to love her.

**Fiona Wall  (12)**
**Parkstone Grammar School**


# The Lonely Ship

As it majestically sweeps the lonely sea,
Like a graceful dove gliding through the sky,
The glorious ship, tall and proud,
Sails to an unknown mystic island,
For nobody knows the enclosed power and glory,
The raging sun reflects on the rippling water,
Like God reaching down his hand,
As if to guide the ship along the isolated sea,
The calmness and peace seems unreal,
Like the starless orange sky above,
The waves part and the dolphins jump grandly,
Who may drive this ship of dreams?
Is this vision true
Or is it just a figure of my imagination?

**Dannielle Cox  (12)**
**Parkstone Grammar School**

# The Rainy Day Prison

The rain made a snail trail on the windowpane,
It slid slowly down the glass,
Spreading right and left like tree branches
And cascading into puddles below.

She peered through the dull mist, longing for the sun,
Dreaming of ice cream and hot summer days,
Summer meadows and warm breezes
And children's laughter to illuminate her surroundings.

A rumble of thunder interrupted her thoughts
And lightning lit the sky,
She wished on her lonely soul,
The storm would cease and blow away.

Then her wish for the sun was granted,
The clouds parted and blue sky appeared,
Unlocking her from the rainy day prison,
Allowing her to break free and frolic in the sunshine.

**Leanne Columbine  (13)**
**Parkstone Grammar School**

# Inside . . .

Inside the peacock's eye, the glistening sun,
Inside the glistening sun, a solar eclipse,
Inside the solar eclipse, the sticky, humid air,
Inside the humid air, a dark, damp night,
Inside the dark night, a scary nightmare,
Inside the scary nightmare, a never-ending tunnel,
Inside the tunnel, a multicoloured coral reef,
Inside the coral reef, a rippling wave,
Inside the rippling wave, a forgotten memory,
Inside the memory, an unsolved mystery,
Inside the mystery, a brewing thunderstorm,
Inside the thunderstorm, a circle of quiet voices,
Inside the quiet voices, the peacock's eye.

**Stacey Osmond  (13)**
**Parkstone Grammar School**

# Imagine

Millions of people from every race
Smiles spread widely over every face
No one can touch them or bring them down
Because love, peace and freedom are all around

People breathing in through their eyes and ears
Mesmerised by what they see and hear
Deep oceans stretch out blue and clear
The sound of silence eases their fears

No disease litters their lives
No thoughts of evil scar their minds
No tyrant figure decides their fate
No need to run away, no need to escape

Within this world the people are free
Friendships formed with those overseas
Sunlight beams across the sky
There is no need to fantasise

Millions of people from every race
Smiles spread widely over every face
No one can touch them or bring them down
Because love, peace and freedom are all around.

**Bryony Greenfield  (14)**
**Parkstone Grammar School**


# Golden Eye

The great golden eye watched,
The waves splashing against the yellow stern,
As the whirling current danced laughing,
The great vessel displaced the surface,
Many larger and smaller waves followed,
That were liquid and uneven,
As the stately and rapid ship
Made its way through the great golden sea.

**Emma Porter  (12)**
**Parkstone Grammar School**

# Hope

Hope seems such a small word,
Yet on it we all depend.
Hope stays with us every day
And will to the very end.

Hope is love,
Hope is joy.
Hope's a lifesaver,
But don't treat it like a toy.

Hope's there when you need it,
To help you through the day.
Showing you and guiding you,
Persuading you to stay.

Always hold on to your hope,
For the time will come, you see.
We all need a little hope,
In our times of need.

Hope seems such a small word,
But on it we all depend.
Hope stays with us every day
And will to the very end.

**Emma Guy (14)**
**Parkstone Grammar School**


# The Sea

The sea was like a large eagle
Hovering over the land
Waiting for its prey
To scurry over the sand
Then it dived out of nowhere
And flew along the shore
It then reached back
And hovered once more.

**Tiggy Burrows (12)**
**Parkstone Grammar School**

# The Sea Cat

Our little boat in a blazing storm,
Like a cat playing with a ball.

The waves hit the sides,
The cat hits the ball.
The thunder rolls overhead,
The owner plays a drum.

Our little boat in a blazing storm,
Like a cat playing with a ball.

With a swoosh of wind,
A flick of the tail.
The boat starts to tip,
The ball rolls along.

Our little boat in a blazing storm,
Like a cat playing with a ball.

A flash of lightning,
The house lights are on.
The rain pours down,
The cat begins to cry.

Our little boat in a blazing storm,
Like a cat playing with a ball.

The storm grows calm,
The cat goes to sleep.
The wind whistles past,
The cat starts to purr.

Our little boat in a blazing storm,
Like a cat playing with a ball.

**Katie Morris  (14)**
**Parkstone Grammar School**

# Anger Reigns

The moon shining bright and full,
Yet below the sky anger reigns,
Upon the stormy sea,
Pitching, rolling, tossing, crashing,
Waves break the silent sea.

Crashing waves against the boat,
Helpless we may be,
Our fate decided down below,
Riding on the sea.

Fights between us pushed away,
Friends we all can be,
Pushed together by the storm,
Together on the sea.

So into the fearful night we ride,
My friends, the boat and me,
Hope with hope,
That morn may come,
Peaceful it may be.

In the night the moans and groans,
Carry so easily,
All we wish and all we want,
Is to arrive safely.

The stars twinkling up above,
Keep us all happy,
For they are not affected,
By the troubles of the sea.

**Kirsty Gurney  (13)**
**Parkstone Grammar School**

# The Eagle And Mirror

The eagle, great and blue,
Looked into the mirror of dreams,
There he could see the sunset,
With him over the waters.

He saw himself looking into the mirror
And saw the piercing stare
And sleek, flat, blue feathers,
From himself and admired.

He saw the reflection of all the beach,
But saw it had changed,
No great changes,
But small and sweet.

For one the scenery was covered in reds,
The sun looked like a large tomato glistening,
There was no grey rocky cliffs,
But there was still the long pieces of dried grass.

He tore his eyes away from the mirror
And saw the different shades of blue,
Saw the rippling cool pale sea
And saw the great white clouds.

The eagle, great and blue,
Looked away from the mirror of dreams
And looked at the simmering sun
And flew swiftly over the cool waves.

**Hannah Waring  (13)**
**Parkstone Grammar School**

# Sunset

A glittering reflection,
A sprinkle of clouds,
A line of light,
Sunset.

Old ships passing,
An adventure beginning,
The sea is calm,
Sunset.

A white fire glowing,
A rippling note,
Space is everything,
Sunset.

Freedom is life,
To live is to learn,
Light is magic,
Sunset.

**Anna Ramsbottom  (12)**
**Parkstone Grammar School**


# Darkness

Darkness falls over the small village,
Houses, trees, any other signs of life are now silhouettes,
A storm is heading their way,
Crackles and rumbles, heard from a distance,
But it's getting closer and louder,
*Bang!* The thunder rages and the ground shakes,
Following the thunder is the lightning,
Trickling through the sky,
Flashing different colours, crackling as it moves.
But then silence,
As the storm moves away,
All that can be heard,
Is a distant rumble.

**Lizzie Wheable  (12)**
**Parkstone Grammar School**

# High Tide

The sea is like a hungry lion
Picking out its prey
Restless until it devours the wind
And folds over upon itself

A slippery snake
Slithering amongst the coral
Baring teeth
A sharp blade of hurt and betrayal

An icy void
Amongst the shipwrecks
A thousand years to tell
Wrapped in an untouchable rainbow

A pearl of wisdom
An arm of comfort
Washing over us
Pulling us close

A graceful butterfly
Flitting to and fro
Reflecting the sunlight
As it reaches out to touch the clouds

Like a child's playmate
Sealing precious memories
Frolicking and hopeful
Glinting eyes awake with truth

The sea is . . . another world.

**Elizabeth Jackson  (13)**
**Parkstone Grammar School**

# The Magical Man

The stench of popcorn rides on the breeze
Glaring lights illuminate his stage
The mob buzzes, eager for a glimpse
Of this magical man
His face haunts the papers
But there is another face, another name
One not spoken nor seen
A small figure, limp and fragile
Lies crumpled in the shadows
Big, empty eyes stare out
As tears drip onto the parched earth
This child is starving too
But for him there is no fame
No cameras record his suffering
No front page for his hunger
No chance to leave his own box of pain
No choice for this child
For the magical man
The end comes with bright lights and applause
For the nameless boy
The end comes only with darkness
And a deep, eternal slumber.

**Lauren Curley  (16)**
**Parkstone Grammar School**

# Freedom

The sunset glows over the calm sea
It makes it glisten and sparkle
As each gentle wave takes a droplet of sunshine
And reflects it perfectly

A ship floats peacefully on the waves
Bound for the everlasting horizon
A journey of adventure
Through the land of forgotten dreams

The sky is scattered with orange and gold
The sun is a copper coin
So relaxed, so tranquil
Yet vibrant and beautiful

The graceful ship glides towards the distance
Visionary, with a dreamlike quality
As if an enchanting spell has been cast over it
Crowned with splendour it travels on

How wonderful to be sailing on that elegant ship
Imagine . . . absolute bliss!
Just you and the world
On a romantic voyage to freedom.

**Alicia Wright  (12)**
**Parkstone Grammar School**

# Indian Bear Dancing

He trains sloth bears to dance
To make them jump up and prance
Who's he kidding?
He takes all the winnings
Using needles is torture
Think of that poor creature
Bears suffer with pain
His owner must be insane
Red-hot needles go in and out
Then rope is forced through, bears scream and shout
Now owners pull teeth out, they are being fools
They don't use anaesthetic and use blunt tools
Whips and metal oh so cruel
Using force that's how they make them move
If only they set sloth bears free
When owned by a kalander or a gypsy, bears die 17 years early
WSPA is trying to sort it out
Telling tourists not to give money, it doesn't help the bears out
3,000 rupees are earned a month
It's not fair, enough's enough!

**Jodie Elmer  (12)**
**Parkstone Grammar School**

# A Troubled Young Mind!

'My name is Jim,' I said,
As I lay awake in bed.
My hair is curly, glasses round
And something else that I have found,
Is everyone else is big and tall
And I'm the smallest of them all.
I somehow always look ahead,
To the time when I am gone and dead.
Everyone says I'm four, how silly,
But I know I'm rising five, it's easy.
I dream of the time when I'm grown up,
It'll be so much better when I'm grown up.
*But what then?* I think to myself,
Marriage, kids and wealth
And after that, what will come?
A year or two and I'll be gone.
So how on earth can I enjoy
This time while I am a small boy?
With these thoughts all in my head,
I lay back down and went to bed.

**Natasha Scotson  (12)**
**Parkstone Grammar School**

# Terror In The Eyes Of Freedom

The audience gathers,
I'm in a restrain.
While they laugh and joke,
I am in pain.

One cowboy comes up
And pulls at my head,
'I won't have that saddle put on,' I said,
But they didn't listen and once it was on,
He jumped on my back, the gate opened
And we were gone.

This game is fun,
As everyone heeds,
The cowboy is smiling,
Whilst the horse bucks and bleeds.

I hear a great noise,
Like the dust in my ears.
I scream and I whinny,
The audience cheers.

What is the point of this panic and plunder,
I try to throw him, but my legs crumple under,
Then I'm on the ground, snorting with fear,
Whilst not one of the crowd sheds even a tear.

When the cowboy's the champion of the show,
Everyone loves him, they all say so.
'He's great! He's good! We all know.'

So when it's time to say, 'goodbye',
I think of my loved ones as in the dirt I lie,
I hear them scream, praising the man,
Who killed the horse that eats wheat and bran.

They scream, they cry, 'He's a hero!' they lie,
Whilst far away in the background,
I let my body die.

**Emily Knights (13)**
**Parkstone Grammar School**

# Gulf War Words

To fight the terror from land, sea and air,
Were the words that came from Bush and Blair.
Despite the calls for time and patience,
They ignored the wishes of the United Nations.

We must invade and bring down the reign,
Of the evil madman Saddam Hussein.
So you searched with spy planes and satellites too,
But to this day he has still escaped you.

So has the man gone, have we righted a wrong?
But why has the shooting lasted so long?
And why have the people with faces so haunted,
Not come to praise us, is it not what they wanted?

Weapons they said of mass destruction,
Have only lead us to civil disruption.
What was it for, to set free the land
Or seize control of the oil 'neath the sand!

**Dave Hunter  (15)**
**Portchester School**


# Fate

Fate can't be controlled in any way,
Something that happens
That's there to stay,
It won't go away.
Fate was World War II,
It effected me and you.
Fate controls our destiny,
Maybe a bit of intensity,
It paves the way for society.
It could be now or then,
You never know when.
It's fate
And you can't set a date.

**Marco Goisis  (14)**
**Portchester School**

# Waiting To Die

He sits there waiting,
Waiting to die
What has he done?
He doesn't die for how he is,
He dies for what he believes.

They laugh as they watch him die,
Every day growing weaker,
Slipping in and out of sleep,
As he thinks what they have done,
To his family and friends.

They laughed as his wife was shot,
They laughed as his children cried,
Blood dripped from the wall,
His dog lay in a woolly heap,
He couldn't stop the soldiers.

He had said things,
Things they didn't think was right,
He thought thoughts,
Thoughts they didn't like,
He wanted to die, he was waiting to die.

He lay on the floor,
Closed his eyes and prayed,
Prayed for death,
He hoped he would see his family,
He took his last breath and died.

This man is one of many,
Killed for what they believe,
Open your eyes and see,
What is all around you
And help change it.

**Matt Roberts (14)**
**Portchester School**

# Are We Remembered?

Through fallen the fallen bodies and long-lost souls,
In flows the storm as the slumbering sky twists and rolls,
Containing a free-flowing hatred with one dirt stained palm,
Fear subsides for there is no longer any danger of harm.

Trudging the trails laid through open fields of destruction,
A plague upon men for stirring this unholy concoction,
Great warriors lie silent as decent men cry out,
Whispers of their last moments echo like an amplified shout.

Rising from the red mud with a black sun teasing charred skin,
The final stand of an ancient battle, still with no means
with which to win,
Echoing prayers and whispered screams coat the morning air,
A fallen priest clutches a bloodied crucifix with undying despair.

Voices grace the softening tide while aged memories are drawn
from deep within,
Ancient wounds re-opened again to once more burn
with forgotten sin,
The shadows of time cloak each corpse and mask its true face,
But who would know when to consider and value each
condemning pace?

In the skies above lingers a purifying light slowly cleansing
stained limbs,
Celebrations of pride and victory follow commemorative
prayers and hymns,
But as the gaping wounds cease up and reveal careless defeat,
Expressions of stolen pride are obvious and indiscrete.

As fate confronts the lost souls and provides their release,
The feelings of hope and stubborn pride refuse to cease,

But as those with valour are consummately dismembered,
Silenced voices question, 'Are we remembered?'

**Ryan Head  (16)**
**Portchester School**

# Those Chosen Few

Shut your eyes and think way back,
To when Britain's air force didn't crack,
Remember those pilots, those chosen few,
Killing as a living to see the day through.

Open your eyes and look into the sky,
This was their battlefield way up high,
They fought with all their strife,
So the future generation could have better life.

They saw many of their friends die,
So killing the enemy was their reply,
For us to speak English today,
Their life was the sacrifice they had to pay.

Now bow your heads for those men without fear,
They need a thank so let's give them a cheer,
The price that those brave men paid,
Was the biggest sacrifice anyone could have made.

**Nathan Dawes  (14)**
**Portchester School**


# Right From Wrong

I don't think it is right
That dads pull pints
Because it never does the youngsters any good

What do they do
When they see their dads in the loo
Being sick like there's no tomorrow?

They follow what they have done
Because they think it is a load of fun
Until they find themselves in hospital

We should teach these guys a lesson
To stop their kids from depression
So they can lead a normal life.

**Christian Meade  (14)**
**Portchester School**

# My Girl

Compared to the lips you have,
The rose means nothing to me,
Your hair makes golden sand
Look like pale winter's deception and
Love of killing all things pure and warm,
Loving and kind.
Compared to the heart you have
The sea cannot be vast enough
To fill this loving muscle,
That beats in my mind all day,
All night, like an endless fountain of love,
For all things true and beautiful.
Compared to your secretive eyes,
Mine seem like rotten fruit,
All shrivelled up and lifeless,
No force of man or nature could tear me away
From your radiant beauty,
That brightens the very rain clouds
On a rainy day.
Compared to you,
I am an ugly monster with no features of love or compassion,
Only the love and compassion I have for you.

**Thomas Daubney (12)**
**Portchester School**


# Fear

As the rumble draws closer the civilians run faster,
With all guns poised waiting for the enemy's martyr,
Coming round the corner in an armoured tank,
When we saw their army all our hearts sank,
Now fighting a lost cause we all looked to flee,
But I wait for my bullet to come and find me . . .

**Lee-Paul Chapman (15)**
**Portchester School**

# Monday Mornings

I woke in my bed,
With a drowsy head,
Not wanting to go to school.
I clung to my pillow
And scrunched in a ball,
Awaiting the dreaded call.

I turned to look at the time,
But what was the point,
I knew it was 6.59.
The alarm clock rang,
The morning birds sang,
Oh why is it 6.59?

I heard footsteps coming nearer,
Images of school getting clearer,
As I lay in my bed,
With horrid thoughts in my head,
My peaceful night
Was nearly over.

**David Harvey  (14)**
**Portchester School**


# I Hate Poems

I hate poems
And poems hate me
But I wrote this poem
For my homework you see
If you do not like it
At least I can say
That I did my homework
So have a nice day.

**Freddie Coleman  (15)**
**Portchester School**

# Computers

Computers are the way of the future,
We all have one in our house,
We talk to people across the globe,
With the buttons on the mouse.

There are gigabytes and kilobytes,
You can save and delete,
Type letters with the keyboard,
Then you can print when they're complete.

You can put files on a CD,
Or put them on a floppy disk,
You can go on to a program,
To write up your shopping list.

Computers are the way of the future,
We all have one in our house,
We talk to people across the globe,
With the buttons on the mouse.

**Liam Kittle  (14)**
**Portchester School**


# Strange Feeling

It's a strange feeling love, impossible to describe,
It makes you flutter, tingle and glitter inside,
As soon as the person catches your eye,
Out of the window do all the world's troubles fly,
Nothing else matters to you except this,
If you've never experienced it, it's not one to miss!

**Daniel Jeffries  (14)**
**Portchester School**

# There Was A School Boy

There was a school boy,
Who worked and worked,
His friends all called him a jerk,
All he did was work all day
And never any time to play,
One day when walking home,
He was all alone,
Some bullies, they did call,
To try to catch another fool,
But this boy was far too wise,
To listen to the bullies' cries,
The bullies chased across the field,
He found a bush, his only shield,
The bullies threw sticks and stones
And even tried to break his bones,
He snuck away in a silent way
And lived to fight another day.

**Sean Mills  (12)**
**Portchester School**


# War Poem

War is the pointless fight for more and more land.
War just means suffering and pain.
War causes so much unhappiness.
Why do people fight?
Why can't everyone just get along?
What good comes out of war?
Why doesn't the world live in peace?
What would a peaceful world be like?

**Gareth Souter  (14)**
**Portchester School**

# The 'Waiting' Day

Light of dawn calls forth the shepherds morn
To prize open the vision of a day anew
And awake the circle of life once again.
Calm, the shifting waves of water blue
Paddle on the low ground.
But sun a-blinding shines through to start the coloured storm
Crying on the hospital bed
Born a babe of gold,
Then find people's worn and torn of age
Snuggled in slumber.
Look to a window with a gaze
On morning dew and a rose garden of purest rouge
Where the slash of thorn to flesh pours life
Of these many, eventually to earth.

**Kit Moulding  (13)**
**Portchester School**

# The Crop Field

Rigamortis to complexion, by the years of rusted fells
Mortal life a mere illusion, as you're bred inside this cell

Neck snapped back yet holding by a thousand weeping veins
Hearts are blown to fragments, feed the children of the wame

This system feeling for you, your hope, anger and fears
Spineless automatons raising metal to your tears

Take time through we wonder, how departure come to pass
Yet little do we know that we are barely blades of grass.

**Dan Curtis  (16)**
**Portchester School**

# Love By An Arrow

As I looked into her eyes,
I knew it was true,
I was in love,
My heart never lies.

My love grows,
With each passing day,
I never thought it was possible,
To love someone this way.

I love her too much,
Than words could ever say,
Love by an arrow,
Bringing us closer each day.

**Dipak Patel (14)**
**Portchester School**


# Despair!

So you're fed up with life,
Hate and all the strife.
Where did they go wrong
Hiroshima, the bomb?
Vietnam, napalm,
It didn't do you any harm
Iraq? Saddam Hussein;
It'll only happen again.
The world's full of despair,
We never get anywhere.
Surely there must be another way,
To solve the problems of today.

**Daniel Hunt (14)**
**Portchester School**

# Inside Out

I look up at the stars,
then I look at the reflection in the sea,
I wonder what they are
and what they could be.

I know we're not alone in this galaxy,
some of my family are up there looking down on me,
trying not to shed a tear when reminded of them,
all of us knowing what it feels like,
but we just act like men.

Being alone, sat in my room,
staring out of my window, hypnotised by the moon,
I look away from the hurt and hang my head in shame,
because I know one man can make a difference,
am I to blame?
I can't help feeling sorry, but I can't change the way I am,
when I look back at what's gone on,
I've just got to be a man.

I feel really scared knowing anyone can die,
people asking me where they have gone,
and me always having to lie.

I still believe in God, but I know he's punishing me,
I think I've done something wrong,
but I want to know what it could be.

Now as I finish this off, trying to be me,
all my hurt has gone,
now I can start to feel happy.

**Kieran James (13)**
**Portchester School**

# The Poet In The Modern Age

If you want creative writing,
Read the Government reports,
You can see the television,
But the signal will distort.

Battleships confide in me
And tell me where you are.
They've got more than we have,
So let's all start a war.

Di-glycerides of fatty acids,
Help keep your soul in line.
When we ordered them beneath the trees,
How they began to whine.

Atkins has it strengths,
Faith in God does not.
I know you want to be better,
But your soul begins to rot.

We slowly fade out,
As we dance upon the moon;
A swine in a cage,
Mesmerised by the tune.

So much wrong,
But we daren't say,
Lost child at the front desk,
Won't receive its way.

**Daniel Barrow  (14)**
**Portchester School**

# Monday To Friday

Monday to Friday a stressful week
But yet it's made me stronger
As I stare into the night sky
Full of infamous stories
As I look into my brother's eyes
I ask to know more please
As my mother's tear falls
As my heart calls
No reply is my fear
Now forever more my tear is falling
Calling now for salvation
Pleading for a vacation
As I pick up a knife
Willing to end my life
Ringing as the phone is calling
Now my life is hanging
My father's on the other end
Now I turn insane
But he says he's alright
Once more I stare into the night
Until it happens again
Forever I live in pain
It never rains on me just pours
As my soul soars
As death knocks on my door
Once more I call for salvation
My life I'd rather not mention
All I have left is depression
I have a confession
I fear myself more
Than anyone else
I'm digging myself a ditch
As I hitch a ride to the other side
That died a long time ago
To see that person once more
Believe in your dreams . . .

**Ry Mc Atear  (14)**
**Portchester School**

# The Last Breath

The soldier lay among the dead,
Looking up at the sky above,
It is grey and dismal, but in some way calming,
Vibrations of blasts can be felt from afar,
The air is damp, the stench immense,
He fought for his country and all that is right,
He battled hard, from dawn till dusk,
But now he lay still and peaceful,
His eyes slowly close, as he drifts away . . .

**Mark Caunter (14)**
**Portchester School**


# A Light At The End Of The Tunnel

Red is evil, staring down at you,
Red is darkness, screaming boo,
Red is hate, your worst fear,
Red is anger, always really near,
Red is pain, cutting with a knife,
Red is death, the lack of life.

Blue is frost, a shivering thought,
Blue is sad, feeling like you're nought,
Blue is gloom, a shadow over you,
Blue is cold, like there's nothing to do,
Blue is loneliness that makes your soul quiver,
Blue is depression that curls up and withers.

Yellow is brightness, that lights up your life,
Yellow is sunlight, which shines with all its might,
Yellow is warmth, chases the cold away,
Yellow is stars, never seen by day,
Yellow is joy, never lets you fall,
Yellow is happiness, a love for all!

**Alix Ramelli (12)**
**St Mary's CE Middle School, Dorset**

# The Magic Box

*(Based on 'Magic Box' by Kit Wright)*

I will put in the box . . .
The sound of a crocodile snapping
The smell of aftershave
The taste of ice melting on my tongue

I will put in the box . . .
The touch of a cat
The sight of a mountain
And all the animals of the jungle

I will put in the box . . .
A howl of a lion and a roar of a wolf
A screech of a giant panda
And a bamboo-eating monkey

I will put in my box . . .
A sting of a deer
And a scatter of a wasp

My box is made from shark skin
With lion paws
Its locks are shark's teeth

I shall use my box
As a remote control car
And drive into mouse holes.

**Dominic Nicholls (12)**
**St Mary's CE Middle School, Dorset**

# Hedgehog

Hedgehog began
He took a needle from the sewing box
He took the point from a spear
And made his coat

For his eyes
He took two pins from a pin box
He took the colour from the rainbow
And made his eyes

For his nose
He took a chocolate button from the shop
He took a small, wrinkly walnut
And made his nose.

**Gavin Barker  (12)**
**St Mary's CE Middle School, Dorset**


# Winter

What is the meaning of frosty cold days?
When birds are shivering in the bare trees,
People look forward to the warmth of May,
Fallen leaves swirl in a rustling breeze.
Silvery webs shimmer in the bright sun,
A whitening frost covers the hard ground,
Animals asleep wait for spring to come,
A stillness and silence is all around.
Everything is gripped in winter's vice,
The sky is filled with flakes of white snow,
Rivers are frozen by malicious ice,
Pink-cheeked children play in winter's glow.
A million icy diamonds reflect light,
As snowy, freezing daytime becomes night.

**Wyn Bellis  (12)**
**St Osmund's CE Middle School, Dorchester**

# Prophecy

A twisted mind,
A spell of hate,
An evil soul,
That lies in wait.

A rocky shore,
No dusk nor day,
A traveller's doom,
'The Devil's Way'.

A single saviour,
No sign of sin,
Yet haunted by
The dark within.

With legendary weapons,
Spells and songs,
He must craft the justice,
For which he longs.

If goodness stops
And evil starts,
All hopes and dreams
Will tear apart.

If life continues,
So does light,
But only one
Can set things right.

Just one can find
The boy we need:
To help us fight
He must succeed.

**Gabriel Byrde-Yarham  (11)**
**St Osmund's CE Middle School, Dorchester**

# Dreams Sonnet

I drift away on a big fluffy cloud,
When I sleep I only dream about you,
It's my personal space quiet not loud,
In my dreams it is always somewhere new,
One, two, three, how many sheep can you count?
I dreamt a dream the other night,
In my dreams my problems I can surmount,
Before I sleep my mother says, 'Sleep tight.'
In colours vivid and in black and white,
In comfort and in warmth I am wrapped,
Sometimes it's bad, sometimes I have a good night.
Dreams are like a road already mapped,
Some dreams are slow in pace, others snappy,
So long as I have dreams, I am happy.

**Sophia Lucas  (12)**
**St Osmund's CE Middle School, Dorchester**


# Age And Youth

Age and youth can't live in unity,
Youth is a freshly-picked raspberry, age is a wizened old pear,
Youth like health embodied, age like premature baby
                              with no immunity,
Youth like blossoming flower, age like tree blown bare,
Youth is feeling the best, age is failing the test,
Youth is tomorrow, age is yesterday,
Youth is fast and wild, age is slow and mild,
Youth is the bright colours of May, age is tired, old and grey,
Age I hate you, youth I love you!

**Natasha Lummes  (12)**
**St Osmund's CE Middle School, Dorchester**

# A Morning To Remember

In the morning, the city awakes,
The stalls in the market are setting up,
Streamlines of cars are now overflowing,
Delivery lorries are hours late,
Tescos is open, with fresh stock in,
Bakers are icing, butchers are cutting,
The pressure is on for the people's sake,
Curtains open then faces appear,
Factories and traffic pump out fumes,
Shops now open, people flocking in,
Then two bombs go off, the city breaks down,
People complain, things are turned upside down,
In the morning the city awakes,
In the morning the city now flakes.

**Tom Prior  (12)**
**St Osmund's CE Middle School, Dorchester**


# Wolves

There they stand, the noble and grand,
Glaring intently and strong.

The night has closed and the moon has dozed,
For now his time has come.

The wolves are hushed as the night is rushed,
Their hearts as a beat of a drum.

An innocent hare is caught in a snare
And instantly trapped in a scrum.

Their jaws snip and their claws rip,
As supper has come and is done.

As dawn draws near the howls disappear,
Waiting for night to come.

**Nancy Daniell  (13)**
**Sherborne School For Girls**

# Christmas

As I gaze out the window one winter eve,
Watching the droplets of snow,
Making a carpet of whiteness all around
And sparkling in the dim moonlight.

The sound of happiness and laughter,
As the chime of Christmas strikes,
I look closely up in the sky for the reindeers followed by
                                        Father Christmas,
No one to be seen.

The glistening Christmas tree,
Sitting plumply in the large window,
Covered in sparkly golden baubles,
With presents all sizes squished together like Smarties in a tube.

The sweet smell of Christmas pudding whiffs up the stairs,
Reminding me of that true Christmas feeling
And just imagining Christmas pudding with a dob of brandy butter,
Makes my stomach rumble.

I creep downstairs without waking a sole,
From a distance I can see that he did come,
My large sock is waiting stuffed with gifts,
Bulging out the top.

As Christmas comes to an end,
We wait for another year to pass,
The turkeys to fatten,
The trees to grow,
To thank Father Christmas and farewell to the snow.

**Charlotte Tongue  (13)**
**Sherborne School For Girls**

# Mental Strife

Wandering ceaselessly of its own accord,
Up, down, around,
Never pausing,
Wandering still, wondering ever.

Viewing everything,
Nothing escaping,
Fear surrounding,
Wandering still, wondering ever.

Moods veering giddily,
Ever unpredictable,
Feelings tossing like stormy weather,
Wandering still, wondering ever.

Like a raptor stalking prey,
Prowling through darkened rooms,
Always questing, always hoping,
Wandering still, wondering ever.

Undeciding, then certain,
Scurrying as a mouse,
Now fearful, now brave,
Wandering still, wondering ever.

Seizing every moment,
Drawing closer, retreating further,
As a cat always alert,
Wandering still, wondering ever.

Wandering ceaselessly of its own accord,
Up, down, around,
Never pausing,
Wandering still, wondering ever.

**Lucy Cantrell  (13)**
**Sherborne School For Girls**

# At The Speed Of Light

Wind forcing my head back,
Petrified, scared and afraid,
At the speed of light.
Bouncing up and down,
Nearly exiting the saddle.

Dead foot,
Numb leg,
Fingers frozen to the spot.
Wobbling, swaying,
Halfway off.

Ground swirling round and round,
Green everywhere mixed with brown,
At the speed of light,
Falling, crashing, contact,
Lightning flashes through my head.

**Emily Palmer  (12)**
**Sherborne School For Girls**


# Falling Through A Bottomless Bucket Of Nothing

I'm falling through a bottomless bucket of nothing
And the blood is beginning to rush to my head.
I'm getting quite chittery and chattery and chilly,
I'm starting to wish I were back in my bed.
I'm falling through space and I'm swinging and swaying,
I don't think I'm able to keep myself steady.
I'm getting quite woozy and wonky and weird,
If there was a bottom I'd never be ready.
I'm falling through nothing, but nothing is nothing,
So surely I'm not really falling at all.

**Eleanor Simpson  (12)**
**Sherborne School For Girls**

# My Sister's Ocean

Her big bright eyes stared straight into my heart
They poured out love and slowly built an ocean
An ocean so deep I drowned instantly
An ocean so wide I knew I'd never cross

When I held her close I felt her heartbeat
I kissed her cheek that one last time
That next morning
That next cloudy morning I was standing on ground
The ocean around me was no longer there

The angel they called 'Death' had taken her from me,
The angel of death had taken what was mine.
My heart overflowed with grief,
But I knew that one day,
One day as bright and beautiful as her eyes,
I'd be swimming once again in my sister's ocean.

**Lucy Muluzi  (12)**
**Sherborne School For Girls**


# Under The Sea

Millions of colours flooding my vision,
Blues, silvers, reds and yellows,
As soon as they see me they dive down into the deep,
Only emerging when I'm out of sight.

Seaweed rippling in the current,
As though it is cobwebs in the wind.
All different sized bubbles floating to the surface
And breaking at the top.

**Katherine Bayley  (12)**
**Sherborne School For Girls**

# Scuba-Diving

I took the air tank,
It was incredibly heavy,
I plunged into the waters,
It became as light as an oxygen bubble.

Shoals of fish were flittering,
In and out of the coral,
The sea was as warm as hot sand
And I could feel the sun on my back.

Big fish, small fish, coloured fish and spotty fish,
They were all there,
Shimmering like a mirror for a few seconds,
Then darting away.

The coral was right underneath me
And then it dropped down,
Way beneath me,
Into the deep fathoms of the sea.

**Katie Maidment  (12)**
**Sherborne School For Girls**


# Colours Of Nature

Grey as the clouds in the middle of winter,
Blue as the ocean that laps the balmy beach,
Red as the sky on a mid-summer's night,
Golden-brown leaves as they go *crunch, crunch, crunch*,
White as the snow on the Christmas slopes,
Orange as the sunrise on a spring morning,
Green as the grass in the mid May pastures,
Black as my mood on a stormy day,
Yellow as the sun in the sandy desert,
Wonderful colours that whirl around in my head,
Kaleidoscope colours of nature so easy to find.

**Annabel Ricketts  (11)**
**Sherborne School For Girls**

# Autumn Winds

Summer has loosened her gentle hand,
A stronger arm grips the land,
Rustling and whistling,
Winding and weaving,
Autumn winds are crossing the land.

Galloping, cantering, we sail the hills,
Walking through, past fields, ponds and mills,
The world is dying,
The world is crying,
I hear her song o'er the hills.

The storms are gathering,
The dark clouds rolling,
My steed shifts with unease,
Trees shudder in the breeze,
Eyeing the black clouds billowing.

Turning her back on the Earth,
Seeing nothing of its worth,
The goddess of the land utters a sigh,
Winds are rolling up on high,
Rain begins to dampen all mirth.

Finally winter grasps the world,
Warm and snug, wild creatures stay curled,
Deadly still,
Down by the mill,
Where my breath before me furled.

We long for summer,
When days are warmer,
To run, gallop by the stream,
When I no longer see the steam
Of winter, of days that were once colder.

**Victoria Bullard-Smith (13)**
**Sherborne School For Girls**

# Bullying

As they approached, a wave of panic gripped me,
I couldn't run, I couldn't hide.
The glare of their eyes rooted me to the spot,
My heart and my head were pounding.
I felt as if thousands of needles were digging into me,
Their breath was icy cold,
It made me shiver as it touched my flesh.
I was lifted off the ground, only hearing nasty, raucous jeers,
Then just to fall onto a hard ground and find my back in agony,
Hearing laughter.
My elbows were grazed and bleeding,
The tears in my eyes were stinging,
'Who's a baby? Who's a mummy's pet?'
Help me someone; take me away from here,
I can't stand it any longer,
Running, running, chasing, chasing,
My head is spinning and I have a stitch,
They are catching up and I can't run much further.
I have to stop, I can't carry on,
A fist and then darkness . . .

**Francesca Tennant (11)**
**Sherborne School For Girls**


# The Golden Eagle

I am king of the sky
As I swoop through the mountains
I flow with the breeze
I cool by the fountains

On my way home
I feel gallant and bold
I follow the sun
My wings turn a glimmering gold.

**Sarah Cripps (11)**
**Sherborne School For Girls**

# My Boat

On the sea in my boat,
I sway from side to side.
Out on deck, I see the dolphins crashing down on each wave.
Then in the distance faintly I see the harbour.
Each boat dipping bow on bow.
I lift the heavy anchor,
I start gliding through the waves towards the dolphins,
Just the silent sea and me.
I see the fish deep down.

The wind suddenly rises,
It's freezing cold.
There is a storm brewing,
The waves crash against the side of the boat.
I have to put down the anchor to be safe; I don't want to risk my life,
Suddenly I feel scared, why am I? I've been through storms before
And I've survived,
I'm on my own.
I sit inside.
It's not silent anymore,
It's the crashing, splashing, really rough waves,
I hate them.

**Serena Lillingston-Price (11)**
**Sherborne School For Girls**

# The Monster

Shiny scales rise from the sea,
Eyes glinting like hellish sunsets,
As roaring like a monstrous thing,
Flame floods forth from its mouth,
Setting the city on fire,
Tears from the sky quench the thirsty flames,
As it turns away with an exultant eye
And darkness swallows the blue.

**Yvonne So (14)**
**Sherborne School For Girls**

# The Cheetah

The cheetah smoothly crept through the grass,
Sneakily he approached his prey,
His legs higher than his body, crouched down,
The dusty grass covering him,
He gets closer and closer, quieter and quieter,
Then pounces.
The sprint, fast and furious,
Dashing through the grass
And then it stops.
Suddenly,
The antelope struggling for its last breath,
The other family members watching, stopped in their tracks,
The cheetah quickly devours the small animal,
Blood dripping everywhere,
Attracting all the hyenas from across the savannah,
Howling and calling for others to come,
The antelope is left for the hyenas to finish up,
While the cheetah sulks off to under a nearby tree,
To look after its small hungry cubs,
It's had a successful hunt,
But will it be so lucky next time?

**Emily Sharland (12)**
**Sherborne School For Girls**


# The Life We Live

Shut your eyes and the scenes still remain,
A view so terrifying it jolts every vein,
Stop your nose and you can still smell the fear,
So far away and yet so near,
Close your ears and the sounds will continue,
All through your life they will never leave you,
Hold on to your hands; you don't want them to feel,
For touch would bring feelings far too surreal,
The life that we live is just one big lie
And while we live it, thousands will die.

**Serena Franklin (14)**
**Sherborne School For Girls**

# The Eagle

There he preens
Upon a nest
Amid lovely scenes
He combs his breast

He sights some prey
Something small and slight
Amid its dray
But great in might

He is no longer grooming
There is food in the air
And he is looming
He will leave nothing spare

This done he sits there in all splendour
He looks good
He's a master blender
The best of the brood

He is honest, he tells no lies
There he is the king of the skies.

**Georgia Stevenson  (12)**
**Sherborne School For Girls**


# Her Pony

Her pony was a dark streak on the hazy moor.
He looked like he wasn't fit to work,
But inside he was the strongest horse I know
And was as loyal to his owner as an old dog to his.

Every day for 20 years he pulled her cart,
It rocked steadily up and down the hazy moor,
Where the purple heather grows onto the horizon
And all this time no one knows where she goes.

**Mieke Dale-Harris  (14)**
**Sherborne School For Girls**

# The Sun Is Rising

The night is nearly over
The moon is sad and sober
But the stars they twinkle on
Until all the dark is gone

The Earth it slumbers too
Beneath the deep, dark blue
And through clouds may pass
The silence seems to last

The air is now light
And horizon comes to sight
The world starts to buzz
In the early morning fuzz

The sun rises in the sky
As the night begins to die
And one by one the birds
Sing out their happy words.

**Annabel Bertie  (14)**
**Sherborne School For Girls**


# On The Jetty

I stand on the jetty and listen!
To the sound of the lapping water rolling back and forth
                                    over the silver shingle.
The mixed smells tingle my nose as I smell fish, ice cream
                                    and suncream
And hear the seagulls call to each other waiting for an
                                    expected drop of feed.
I see a fisherman hand a rope to me,
I realise that he wants me to tie it onto the jetty.
So I twist the wet, slimy, green cord round the cold metal post.
He clambers out of his boat with fishing nets in his hands
And a pipe in his bristly mouth and with a tip of his hat he walks on.

**Alice Evans-Bevan (13)**
**Sherborne School For Girls**

# War Goes On

War goes on, the happiness dies,
Death is sweet on a battlefield,
Then comes a shrill cry of the wounded soldier,
Lying amongst his foe.

The smell of dead and burning flesh,
The sound of wind and fire,
The sad calling of circling birds,
A smoking funeral pyre.

It used to be a place where children used to go,
But now it's a barren wasteland,
Dead bodies everywhere you go.

There isn't any grass or trees,
As there was before the battle.
The sun sets as the bloodshed ends,
Everyone's dead or gone.

Life is strange and short for the brave,
For the one who lives life to the full.

But as his mind shuts down,
He knows his job is done,
He did his best, it wasn't enough,
*We lost* he thought *they won.*

A dark shadow bent over him,
Fire alight in its eyes.
'Your time is done,
Your deed is won and now it is time to die.'

He said a prayer, he closed his eyes,
No one knew his name.

'War goes on, the happiness dies,
Death is sweet on a battlefield.'

**Sophie Mann  (13)**
**Sherborne School For Girls**

# Always In Shadow

Damp enveloped the misty air, still and soundless,
Moist air steeps through grey slatted rock and spongy moss,
Hillocks of grey-yellow nature, pale and placid,
Are scattered on the flat land, speckled with night dew,
Dense fog obscures vision, no life in sight, alone,
Abundant lonely land, forsaken, forgotten
A finger of light sweeps over the dull terrain,
Grey dawn strokes the lifeless moss, swiftly disappears,
Like a shadow, or lost dream that cannot return.
Memories of light and life, just a gentle hum,
A dream, almost forgotten, almost remembered,
Ghostly light is filtered like pale wash over earth,
As the sun wakes up, the world is now awakened,
But the moor is always in shadow, always alone.
Always in shadow.

**Georgina Chapman  (13)**
**Sherborne School For Girls**


# Along The Seashore

When you walk along the shore
The sea breeze through your hair
The sand as soft as the silk of a lady's dress
Weaving in and out your toes
A splash of salty water here and there
You don't know how it feels! Oh how it feels!
The rocks, oh yes the rocks
How they gleam, how they stand up to the raging
Roaring, flaring, falling, wonderful ocean waves
I don't know why, I don't know how
But the caves are dark and slippery
So dim and horribly slimy
They smell of salt and stinking horrible smelling seaweed
But even the caves won't drive me away from my beautiful
Wonderful, extremely colourful, fantastic, blue ocean waves.

**Ellie Morris  (12)**
**Sherborne School For Girls**

# Forever Alone

Alone I sit,
Alone I stand,
Alone I sleep,
Alone I am.

Alone with nature
Forever I'll be,
Alone is my status,
Can't you see?

Sometimes I think
I wonder why,
I can't just leave
And let time go by.

But for now I'm stuck,
So let me be,
To live a life
In captivity.

**Camilla Watson  (13)**
**Sherborne School For Girls**


# The Waves!

The waves crash,
Thunder and splash,
The rocks crumble,
As the beach rumbles.

The dark blue against the bright white clashes,
As the rain lashed down
And broke the sea.

As the clouds went less black,
The sea was flat,
The sea was wild
And not for a child.

**Natasha Lean  (13)**
**Sherborne School For Girls**

# Snow

The snowflakes were gleaming
I sighed and admired the snow
In the air the snowflake twirled
And in the air the snowflakes whirled

I gazed out of the window
And dazzled at the ground
Then watched the soft powder
I opened the latch
And held out my hand

I felt the cold on my face
Then returned to my place
The laughter outside
Brought tears to my eyes
I quietly sighed
And then cried and cried

Nobody was lonely
Nobody was deprived
Nobody was unloved by everyone alive

The anger glared at me
And the snow made me see
How happy I really should be.

**Charlotte Carey (13)**
**Sherborne School For Girls**


# Dream

I had a dream
The dream was about sea
In my dream there were dolphins
Jumping up and down in the sea
In my dream there were crabs
Walking along the horizon and straight onto the beach
I have a clock
The clock woke me up.

**April Liu (14)**
**Sherborne School For Girls**

# The End

He lay in a trance, one of his hands lying in mine.
His see-through skin showing me vast lands
With rivers running around hills and valleys.
His chest rises and falls with the beep of a machine
Somewhere outside the curtains that enveloped us.
I studied his dark eyes, full of wisdom and knowing,
I saw a flicker of pain dance across his face and felt sick.
His healthy, lively body haunted me.
Times when he taught me to ride a bike in the park.
His strong structure holding me firmly.
I remember the autumn leaves dancing happily around us.
I had felt so safe.
*Beep, beep, beep*, went the machine as if it was trying to comfort me.
*Thump, thump, thump*, went my broken heart.
For the last few seconds he looked at me and smiled,
A smile telling me that it would be all right.
A smile to comfort me.
A smile that would be with me in my dreams and nightmares.
A smile of love.

**Charlotte Stuart-Grumbar (13)**
**Sherborne School For Girls**


# The Old Boot

I am smelly and mouldy,
I am dirty and worn down.
I am locked in a cupboard,
To face the smell all on my own.
I smell of mouldy cabbage and
I look like a clump of mud.

My laces are torn and look like bitten straw,
My sole is as thin as paper.
I smell so bad, no one will ever come near me,
It's not my fault I'm an old boot!

**Flora Davidson-Houston (13)**
**Sherborne School For Girls**

# Peace

I'm out in the big wide ocean,
Rolling in the big blue waves.
All I can see is crystal-blue,
All I can hear is the waves at my boat.
Not a piece of land,
Nor a person in sight,
This is peace; this is paradise.

My sails dance in the gentle breeze,
The clear sea twinkles in the evening sun.
I hear birds calling a faint hello,
I see fish come up to catch a glimpse,
This is peace; this is paradise.

I'm off to an island,
Where no one has been.
To buzz with the bees, to sing with birds,
To dance with the butterflies
And to swim with the fish.
All on my own with no one around,
This is peace; this is paradise.

**Caroline Arden (13)**
**Sherborne School For Girls**


# The Meaning Of A Sea Breeze

He stepped out onto the soft white sand
And walked towards a gentle, old hand,
The hand would catch you if you fell,
But the fierce monsters of the underground came to take him to Hell,
But before they could reach him,
The angels of Heaven came to save,
To take his spirit, so he could rest safely in his grave
And as they did, he now could hear the low lapping of the
                                        waves with ease
And with a shudder they took his spirit away with a sea breeze
And now he can rest in peace.

**Alexandra Pawson (13)**
**Sherborne School For Girls**

# Storm

I sit and watch the world go by,
Huddled under dark umbrellas,
The bleak sky is hurling down bullets.
The pearly rain stings the sou'westers,
Leaving singed streaks that gradually fade into oblivion.

The imperial storm closes around the world,
Suffocating,
Grasping,
Controlling.

No earthly vessel can fight through,
This great wall of cloud.
The grey branches of the watching trees billow in fright.
As the cruel wind shouts its laughter
At the participants in this endless race who are bent double in
An unknown effort to win an unknown prize.
The cheating fog takes the trusting slaves captive,
Engulfing them in mile-wide confusion.

**Emily Ayles  (13)**
**Sherborne School For Girls**

# Zambezi River

Two rocks, like grey sentinels, stand on guard,
With the river, a snake, watching his breath,
There's curtains of smoke, yet nothing is charred,
The snake never falling down to his death,
A smooth waterfall roars in the distance,
Over a sentinel's shoulder it lies,
The sheen of water shows no resistance,
To drop to its end, away from the skies.

**Isabel Lockhart Smith  (14)**
**Sherborne School For Girls**

# The Tiger And The Spider

There once was a tiger and a spider,
The spider said please would he hide her,
The tiger's mouth opened wide
And the spider jumped inside
And that was the end of that spider.

They sit together on a lonely peak,
The tiger looks down and he starts to speak,
'Never wander further than the eye can spy,
At the end of that journey, you'll be sure to find.

The thing that made you leave the place you left,
The thing that made your journey quick and deft,
That thing that you would hate to meet again,
That thing 'gainst which you never could defend.

That thing is fear of something near,
Whatever is may be.
Face up to it,
Don't shrink away,
Or it will still forever stay.
It never will depart,
From your fingers,
From your mind
And from your heart.'

**Katie McKenna  (14)**
**Sherborne School For Girls**

# Sherborne School For Girls

S chool is great fun.
H eavily packed with prep.
E mergency fire alarms in the night.
R eading poems in assembly.
B oarding, yes, tuck and all.
O h no maths! I need to do the prep.
R ight, OK, I get that but what about this?
N ever, I don't believe that French is fun,
E verlasting lessons.

S uch hard work to begin with,
C ool dorms.
H ard maths and English,
O verjoyed to go to bed.
O n goes the sidelight to read a book,
L ying in bed trying to get to sleep.

F un games, netball is great.
O h no, I don't like hockey,
R unning round the pitches for a warm-up.

G o! Run! We are late for games,
I am going to be told off.
R ight, what are we doing for games?
L acrosse, I haven't played it before.
S o hard to learn new things.

**Rebecca Collyer  (11)**
**Sherborne School For Girls**

# She

All that she could see,
Was all that she believed,
She didn't try to stop it flowing,
Or change what she conceived.

It's like she was a puppet,
Hanging from her strings,
She was standing alone in her world,
She couldn't change a thing.

She tried to stop this thinking,
Her head it swelled with thought,
She thought as one with nature
And never against it fought.

Her puppet strings, they held her tight,
Restricting her from moving,
The trees, the flowers and the plants,
Couldn't stop their laughing.

They jeered at her through envy,
Through jealousy and spite,
Until she could stand no more of it
And cried with all her might.

She didn't try to stop this,
Facts crowded her belief,
Nothing could come in or out,
As she trembled like a leaf.

All her feelings were crammed inside,
Her spite, her fear and hatred,
Nothing could come in or out,
So away she wasted.

**Heather King (13)**
**Sherborne School For Girls**

# Fame

Walking down the catwalk
Walking up the aisle
Walking down the high street
With your truly dazzling smile

No one can ever dislike you
This you will never regret
For as you are strutting your beauty
You'll win all their hearts, I'll bet

Cameras everywhere you go
Clicking all around
Following you all over town
Until you're homeward bound

You're centre of attention
The world knows your name
Your face is plastered on every wall
Oh the joys of knowing fame!

**Tanya Lawrence  (12)**
**Sherborne School For Girls**


# The Soldier

I am a soldier of a great war,
Terrible things are in store,
For us who have to fight,
Each day and each night.
I am afraid of my friends who shall be lost,
But maybe it is my life that will suffer the cost.

Wandering aimlessly,
Guns shooting all around.
Then suddenly a shock,
I was struck to the ground.
My head was spinning,
Faster than I could think.
Into my heart,
Did that bullet sink.

**Chloë Anderson  (13)**
**Sherborne School For Girls**

# Ponies' Dreams

At night I love to have happy dreams,
About my family of ponies.
We all got together and picked teams
And out came stressy Tony.

Tony was a stable lad,
Who was tall and dark and chatty.
We tried our hardest not to make him go mad,
But in the end he drove us all batty.

The ponies were divided into girls and boys,
When they were only one year old.
To keep them moving they played with their toys,
Which helped them win gold.

When I woke up to go for a ride,
It was always dark and gloomy.
As I sat with great pride,
I always looked like I was zooming.

The horses' other friends were the dogs,
Who always barked and barked.
Together all day they would jump the logs,
All around the park.

My dreams were wonderful until I woke up,
My days were never the same.
At breakfast I dreamed into my cup,
It made life seem very tame.

**Alice Russell  (12)**
**Sherborne School For Girls**

# Little Things Are Best

As I sat and watched
The world go by,
In on the wind
Came a butterfly.

It landed on a ledge
And fluttered its wings,
What would life be
Without these things?

As I sat and watched
The world flow past,
A ship sailed by
With a flag on its mast.

Skimming across the waves
As the ocean sings,
What would life be
Without these things?

As I sat and watched
The world move round,
Children ran and skipped
With a leap and a bound.

Tumbling about
As the school bell rings,
What would life be
Without these things?

**Vicky Simon  (14)**
**Sherborne School For Girls**

# Moonlight

I look up at the stars,
What do I see?
I see the bright moon,
Shining down on me.

The moon is a wanderer,
Roaming the skies,
Watching the ant so small
And the owl so wise.

It ripples down rivers
And shines through trees,
It travels the world
And controls the seas.

But when the day comes,
The moon disappears
And I'll wait for the night-time,
When the wanderer reappears.

**Annabel Bond  (13)**
**Sherborne School For Girls**


# Weakened

She climbs only to fall in return.
She smiles only to cry back.
She gets up only to be rooted.
She looks only to be blinded.
She searches only to be lost.
She strengthens only to be weakened again.
She gains hope only to be shattered and broken.
She stares only to see herself.

**Flora MacInnes  (13)**
**Sherborne School For Girls**

# Do You Know?

Walking down the street, I was stopped by a youth
Who asked this question, 'What happened to you?'

I considered for a moment that lad before me
And wondered if he knew how things used to be.

I sat down beside him and looked in his eyes,
I told him about war but then he just sighed.

I made him stay and began to explain
About the time when many felt pain.

To him I said these words which follow:

'Imagine this you ignorant boy,
Bombs blasting before you and no shred of joy.

Think of people wounded and ill,
Lying alone on a desolate hill.

Smoke filling the air making your eyes sore,
You try to break free but they just fire more.

Stumbling along the trenches deep,
So tired and bruised I began to weep.

I thought of my family whilst all alone
And wished that I could go back home.

Eventually it ended that Great War
And all us men were greeted with awe.'

The boy just sat and stared at the ground,
I lifted his chin, he began to frown.

I said, 'Off you go now,' and he got up,
But before he went he said, 'Thank you very much,

You made me see the truth I never knew.'
And off he went to spread the news.

Now you know about that time
When war was around and how *we* paid the fine.

**Mila Gordon-Creed  (14)**
**Sherborne School For Girls**

# Banished

There was a girl,
Not a normal girl,
But a nothing.

Her name was but a whisper,
That roamed around streets,
Not to be answered.

Her weary feet took steps,
But never met the littered floor,
Yet they were worn.

Her life was a mystery,
Full of tear-jerking memories
That haunted her by shadows.

She lived in a separate world,
One of darkness and fear,
With no sun nor moon.

Her mind was that of a demon's
And a powerful black spirit's,
That led her to do great evil.

This evil was so cruel,
That now she is banished,
Banished from that dark world of hers.

**Sasha Djivanovic (14)**
**Sherborne School For Girls**

# I Have Not . . . But

*(Inspired by a Simon Armitage poem)*

I have not been trekking through the jungle
Where the creepy-crawlies live in puddles
But I have swum in a cool, clear river
When suddenly full of calmness and pleasure.

I have not bungeed off a precipice
Where the stir of the winds is so immense
But I have leant over a cliff and watched
Eagles gliding across a sparkling sea

I have not been there when a crocodile
Has been freed into the fresh, salty lakes
But I have seen four red kites glide swiftly
Through the clear blue air, swooping in the sun

I have not scuba-dived in the Indian Ocean
Where the water is warm and rippling
But I have watched my sister and her friends
Playing when the world has forsaken them

There is a feeling inside that is different
To the rest when you watch someone learning
To overcome the strong chain around them
That jerks them back every time they try to break free.

**Flora Hill  (14)**
**Sherborne School For Girls**

# Stranger

They say she's unspoken of,
A vision only in the distant memory.
She hides in the shadows,
Far away from the light.

No one knows of her,
Just the odd rumour or two,
Who she is
And what she's like:

A princess of a palace,
An angel from the sky.
Or even a monstrous creature
That only comes out at night.

Oh I do want to know
If this rumour is right.
This secretive girl who is nowhere in sight.

**Georgina Cossins  (14)**
**Sherborne School For Girls**


# Jack Frost

Jack Frost is cruel, cold and spiteful,
He creeps over the earth in giant steps,
Breathing ice on cars, roads and lakes,
Coating them in a blanket tough as steel.

He never turns to pity his victims,
Never stops to be kind,
Always on the run,
Coating the world in his mist.

But then the sun comes out, full of pity and kindness,
She turns on Jack Frost
And her rays melt his cold heart,
Not forever, of course, but at least for another year.

**Olivia Eadie  (13)**
**Sherborne School For Girls**

# Winter Night

Darkness swept over the land
Like a sheet of black
The songbirds had spoken
Their last words
And the trees had stopped whispering

Snow lay on branches
Like large wads of wool
The howling wind ceased for a while
Cold filled every corner

The streets were empty
Not a child in sight
Each were in a house
Of glowing warm fires
And some embedded
In a wild land of dreams.

**Cordelia Trasenster  (12)**
**Sherborne School For Girls**


# Autumn

Sitting in the park on a September afternoon
Watching people rush around
Leaves crunching beneath their feet
White clouds from every mouth
A big thick coat, red and gold leaves

My favourite time of the year
Getting exciting as it draws close
Jumping in leaves, splashing in puddles
I love when autumn time is here
Taking a walk on a cold afternoon
Heating and hot chocolate indoors
My hopes are down, excitement drained
It's over and winter here.

**Chantal Bisset  (13)**
**Sherborne School For Girls**

# The Man Who Wasn't There

Footsteps I hear
Close by they are
Pulsing, pulsing,
I stop, I turn, I gaze
But what is that I see?
Nothing, just the blackness of the night

Shadows I see
Close by they are
Darting, darting
As I halt, so do the shadows
Turning briefly to find the source
But the darkness surrounds me once again

Scents now I smell
Close by they are
Haunting, haunting
In fright and protection
I stop, shout and scream
The man who wasn't there is gone.

**Alice Thompson  (14)**
**Sherborne School For Girls**

# A Place For Me

Amid the tall, surrounding palm trees,
Sunlight peeping through the exotic colours,
Luxuriously alone, there she'd be,
On the hump of a graceful camel.

On a breezy bluish day,
She'd crawl among the large sea boulders,
Golden water falling freely,
From the sky and into a steaming lagoon,
The sound so dangerously calming.

Looking down into an isolated village,
Ahead the green, gentle curves of the army of sleeping giants,
With a sea of blue above her,
Would she walk in peace,

Across a sunset beach,
The soft, warm sand collecting between her toes,
The cool, summer breeze rustling through her hair,
There she'd be, alone and free.

**Victoria Ridley  (14)**
**Sherborne School For Girls**

# Water

She rages through the wilderness
And wanders through the trees
Whose skeleton-like branches fall
And she takes them to the seas

She rushes through the darkened caves
Through the dampness and the gloom
She trickled down the gardens
Past the cherry tree in bloom

There's nowhere she can't penetrate
She gives life to all
There's nothing that can stop her
Not rock or tree or wall

Nowhere can withstand her
If she should choose to smite
She can control the human race
She's nature at its height.

**Stephanie Hislop (14)**
**Sherborne School For Girls**


# My Beach

As I walked through the hot, golden sand of the beach,
Memories flooded through my head,
I remembered when I had once played on this beach,
But now others played there in my stead.
I remembered the sensation of sand and sea on my skin,
I tried to rub it off again, along with my kin.
My brothers and I would once play in this sea,
Paddling around and swimming with glee.
I could not feel the sun beating on my back as I could back then,
I could not feel the sand burning my feet,
I decided I would come back to this place often
To enjoy memories of when I lived and watch the people
Enjoy the beach as I once did.

**Samantha Lee (13)**
**Sherborne School For Girls**

# War Is A Dreaded Bore

I never spoke that day, I just cried,
All of my friends and family had died.

There were soldiers everywhere,
There was nothing for me to do, but stare.

The blood stained the ground,
From injured people all around.

At night I sat on my bed,
Instead of music, I heard bombs instead.

The battle went on for days and days,
Everyone was fighting in their own cruel ways.

I was only a small child that day,
So I decided to run far, far away.

There was nowhere for me to go,
Everyone around me was my foe.

I ran for miles and miles in rain and mud,
Not to mention all the red, sickening blood.

At last I stopped running, tears dripping down my cheek,
It was then I realised that the place I was at was rather bleak.

I never knew what happened,
I had obviously been flattened.

I didn't feel myself, I didn't feel alive,
But I knew all I had to do was strive.

So I got up, looked around,
I wasn't even on the ground.

But I knew the place I was in, I could just tell,
The dreaded place that I was in, was *Hell*.

**Jessica Entwisle  (14)**
**Sherborne School For Girls**

# The Ocean – A Dream

My mind wanders through my thoughts,
through music, laughter and memories,
until it stops at the beautiful and entrancing ocean.

The sky is lit by streaks of flashing lightning,
immense claps of thunder rumble passionately
and the great ocean rages and storms beneath.

Great rolling foam-capped waves,
tossing ships high like a bucking horse,
rearing and crashing in a clash of wind and spray.

My mind slips below the raging waves,
out of the noise and light of nature's wrath
and deep into tranquillity and calm.

Playful seals and dolphins frolic amongst each other,
quiet and wise whales glide gracefully past
and colourful fish flit in and out of the coral.

My mind sweeps past shells and drifting seaweed,
past the skeletons where wrecked ships rest,
where mermaids sing soft melodies of joy.

My mind pauses as the creatures tense in fear,
the great white shark terror of all the ocean,
is weaving closer and closer, his tail beating a death beat.

He approaches a small fish unaware of his presence,
his tail beating more and more swiftly,
he opens his powerful jaws and *snap*.

My mind rushes swiftly away,
up into the raging wind and storm
and into the safety of my thoughts.

**Alice Busby (13)**
**Sherborne School For Girls**

# A Skeleton

A rattle,
What was that?
Just on the landing,
It sounded like the cat,
A creak,
A crack
And then even a snap,
I'm scared now,
I'm really, really scared,
What is that?
That thing on the landing?
I don't want to yell 'Mummy',
I want to float away,
I don't like the thing on the landing,
I don't like it at all,
My spine shivers,
A louder creak on the landing now,
It's just outside my bedroom door,
Then my door handle,
I would never have believed it.
But my door handle is moving all on its own,
Or at least I wanted it to be moving on its own,
I didn't want anyone to be on the other side,
I held my breath,
As the door opened I slid under the duvet cover
And as the door creaked open the last few millimetres,
A face appeared,
The face of a
*Skeleton!*

**Zoë Lodge  (11)**
**Sherborne School For Girls**

# When The Sun Goes Down

When the sun goes down
And the moon comes up,
I feel its light on my face.
When the sky gets dark
And the stars light up,
I can stare up into space.
When all the world is bathed in silver
And the people are asleep,
When the lake is alive with sparkling ripples
And all the night animals come out to creep,
When the little moon faeries come out to dance
In their shimmering, glimmering robes
And they dance round and round in a faerie ring,
With their magic silver rings in tow
And with this the night ends
And the faeries retire,
The world begins to awake
And the day starts anew.
In the clear morning sun,
There's a silver ring left down by the lake.

**Mallory Wells  (11)**
**Sherborne School For Girls**

# Stranded

I crawl onto the sand,
The sea lapping around my hands and feet,
The salt soaking into my blood-soaked wound,
Making my leg scream with pain,
I collapse to the ground
And bask in the heat of the sun,
Darkness devours me,
When I wake I see the glistening sea,
The rising sun,
The torn pieces of wood which once were formed into a sea craft,
A ship which has carried me all my life,
I scowl at that treacherous sea,
The sea which I thought I knew and trusted,
The sea which tried to devour me,
Now I am stranded,
No glimpse of a hopeful land breaks, the sight of the cold horizon,
I have been washed up on a strange land,
Glistening sand and a mass of sparkling sea,
I look behind me and see no sign of vegetation,
Dead trees and shrubs I see,
A painful sight,
But I must survive, for I am stranded, alone!

**Sophie Bolesworth  (13)**
**Sherborne School For Girls**

# The Lonely Hunter

As I walked home
From the church at dusk
I saw a shadow
Slip from between the trees
It was a cat
With fur the colour of coal
Thin and coarse
And eyes like hot, glowing amber
He was long-limbed and lean
With a thin, ragged tail
And he looked at me knowingly
As if he could read my thoughts
He was a predator
A lonely hunter
Solitary and silent
Belonging to no one
Wraith-like
He slipped away
Into the darkening night.

**Emily Wiggins  (14)**
**Sherborne School For Girls**

# An Early Morning Swim

The bright clear atmosphere
A blue sky free of cloud
The call of the gulls flying from the cliffs
Remind me of the place I love

The bark of the dog along the cliff
The sharp reprimand of its owner
The tap of the pebbles as they fly from my feet
The rise and fall of the swell

I gasp as the water embraces my feet
I advance steadily on
The water rises to my waist
My arms submerge, I catch my breath

I see the sand below
Through the water cold and clear
The bright morning light shines on my face
Blinding me with a gold flash

I get out now wide awake,
I wrap myself up in my dressing gown,
I look towards the glittering sea,
A fishing boat appears on the horizon,
The bright clear atmosphere.

**Sophy Smith (14)**
**Sherborne School For Girls**

# Memories

A cloud of mist swirls in circles turning the white sky grey,
Lingering behind the sunrise, a wisp of pink is left.
The grass is laden with crisp white powder,
Sheets of ice line the still lake,
A single swan glides across the silk-like waters.

Spices, shouts, bargaining and riches,
Carpets, cloth, fruit and beads,
Wooden stalls full of coloured baskets,
Bunches of wild flowers tied with brown string,
A girl in a corner with a wicker basket swinging it to and fro,
A few pennies scattered at her feet.

Clear blue water rippled as the bow of the boat cuts through the water,
Flitting shapes of colour dart beneath its shadow,
Dragonflies dodge the spray of the waves,
Crickets lull the tropical world to sleep.

Looking down on the terracotta roofs,
Olive trees blossom in the russet soil,
Cathedrals, squares and bustling markets,
The smell of coffee wafting from a nearby café,
The scorching heat beats down on the cobbled street,
Vivid yet ancient these memories dwell,
Whilst the world around me changes they stay clear.

**Emily Mayor  (14)**
**Sherborne School For Girls**

# Holocaust

Dragged away,
Kicked, spat on, punched.
Treated like dirt.
They laugh and kick me to the floor.
'Jewish scum,' they shout.
I don't understand,
I haven't done anything wrong.
They're dragging other people away as well.
My mother, brother and sisters
Have been left till next time though,
Why just me?
Where are they taking us?
My head is bleeding
And my vision has gone all blurry.
But still they keep on hitting me.
They've stopped now,
I lie on the floor,
The grass feels soft and gentle.
Suddenly hauled up to stand in line, I look around,
Everyone facing forward, pale, still,
Saying their prayers.
Gunshots,
Slowly they fall to the ground.
They're coming nearer, I feel as if I'm in a dream,
This is the end.

**Charlotte Diffey  (13)**
**Sherborne School For Girls**

# I Am Not Known To The Entire World

I have not sailed around the world
At an amazing record breaking speed
But I have watched the evening fireflies
Lighting and flitting through the humid air

I have not seen tigers, lions, or the orang-utan
Prowling through the almighty jungle
But I have rowed down a silent river
With nothing but a calming breeze billowing through my hair

I have not swam in the Caribbean
The sheer blue waters dotted with colour
But I have spent a summer's afternoon
Picking cherries from blossom-covered trees

I have not watched eagles soar over the sunrise
Silhouetted by shades of pink
Does tasting the sweetest fruit on your lips
Create the same feeling of harmony?

**Polly Hadden-Paton (14)**
**Sherborne School For Girls**


# First Encounter

Beautiful, she enters my life.
My life has been changed, she, I am attracted.
I look back at her, mysterious.

**Keith Ka-Kei Tse (16)**
**Sherborne School**

# Schizophrenia

Given in love, a promise of a heart:
A sign of things to come;
                    Thrown down with tears, the passing of years
                                Is done: the life is gone.
            The rose feels no conflict.

It gives life to the dying, the magic of man:
His weapon against mortal death;
                    The servant of suffering: no power to help,
                                Only to prolong the pain.
            Good or bad, medicine knows not.

The chance to live dreams, God's gift to man:
The greatest thing we possess;
                    Decay and dementia: the long road to death,
                                And no way of slowing.
            Time gives everything, then takes more.

The key to emotion, the coveted prize
That man seeks above all else;
                    The corrupter of minds, the bait at the end of
                                The road away from God.
            Man seeks knowledge, but knows not its price.

The ultimate end, the fate of us all,
The one certainty of our lives;
                    The key to our passing, the gateway to Heaven,
                                The completion of our earthly test.
            Death can be the end, or a glorious beginning.

Your self usurped by another:
A conflict in your mind;
                    Your self usurped by another:
                                A conflict in your mind.
            The schizophrenic paradox.

**Richard Rabone  (16)**
**Sherborne School**

# Desperation

The wind was howling
through the sails of the
boats on the shore.

The waves lash
against the rocks
forcing cracks in the
rock to expand.

The sight of the
competitors launching
fighting the viscous weather
trying to reach a start.

The 5-minute gun has gone
the wind eating into your
face, desperation building.

The 4th minute has gone
3 minutes left. Adrenaline
gives a new hope after
several swims, 1 minute
to go.

The competitors lining up
what an awesome sight
10, 9, 8, 7, 6, 5 seconds, you're sheeting in
accelerating, 4, 3, 2 seconds
1 second left, your heart is now in
your mouth, you don't want
to mess up, the gun goes, you cross the
line as the gun goes, you're off on
the first leg, fighting 7ft
waves but in the lead.

**Thomas Dunne  (15)**
**Uplands School**

# The Painting

Oh figure of the sweeping hallway,
Are you just a statue of beauty to behold the eye or
Do you have the gift of life?
And strangers of this light passage,
What is your purpose,
In this large entrance to the outside world?
Are you merely just using this building
As an entrance to your purpose
Or is it a place to entertain and to
Converse with your peers?
Indeed it may well be a place of peace
And inspiration, to rejuvenate and to relax.
Do you come here to seek pleasure?
To perhaps enjoy the sight of these statues
Or to wonder, like me, if they are indeed alive?

**Thomas Page  (15)**
**Uplands School**


# A Ringing Phone Must Always Be Answered!

Ringing, ringing, peace suddenly shattered
Who wants to speak to me - what does it matter?
Rushing, rushing quickly to answer
Silence, the sound that fills the air
Who could it be and what is their need?
Is it important or just a small deed?
Should I reply
Or will I fail to comply?
Ringing, ringing, it's a demand
It must be answered as it's in command.

**Richard Griffin  (15)**
**Uplands School**

# Motorway Driving

The pressured wind vigorously pounding through my hair,
The atmosphere so fresh equivalent to a frosty morning,
There was intensified sunshine gleaming down on me,
Like a spotlight concentrating on someone at a pantomime.

On aggressively driving down the intimidating motorway,
Cars were travelling at a horrific speed,
It felt as if you were in the middle of a stampede,
I was incarcerated in the putrid smell of exhaust fumes.

The unremitting amount of filthy cars overtaking me,
They were clambered together like a herd of elephants,
There was an intensive amount of heat surrounding me,
It was like an obnoxious smell hanging around.

The danger made people begin to panic and overheat,
They were like an old-fashioned whistling kettle when boiled,
The steam violently trying to burst out,
Then the sound of brakes screeching as all cars swerve to a halt!

**Wil Robert Whiting (15)**
**Uplands School**


# Night's Sky

I look into the sky at night
And I see its endless darkness.
The moon illuminates the sea to silver
And the stars they shine so brightly.

I look into the sky at night,
The clouds they move so gently
And as the moon's light begins to fade,
The darkness falls upon me.

**Kyle Beesley (15)**
**Uplands School**

# Winter Leaves

Try and change some of the words.
Quickly, it
Came, powerful
And awesome

Our stems, our bodies
Took off from the ground
Acquire the movement

Then it dies
We stop, we stare
People tread us once again

Big feet insist on
Crushing and crunching
The stony floor

It comes again
Our stems, our bodies
Rise up

Twisting, turning
Dodging the people
Flying all around as in

A tumble dryer
We scream and shout
Nobody listens

No one hears
We shout and cry!
We shout and cry!

We are controllable, we are
Sad, we all shout
Nobody listens

Kicking and screaming
In spite of space
Our kind quadruples

We will by nightfall
Inherit mankind
Our bodies on the floor.

**Daniel Bath  (11)**
Uplands School


# The Soul

. . . Where are you?
We need to see you
We crave to see those tranquil eyes staring up at us,
When we walk into a room, to find you sprawled out like a rug.

. . . Where are you?
We need to hear you,
We need to hear your bell jingle
As you shoot downstairs for dinner
And that purr that sends me comfortably to sleep every night.

. . . Where are you?
We need to feel you,
We need to cradle that soft, silky fur
As you fall asleep in our arms.

Please, where are you?
Oh, there you are, and there. Actually, you're everywhere,
You're watching over us just like always,
Except you are no longer body, just purely soul.

But that's just fine because, after all,
What would a body be without a soul?
An exceptional soul, that emerged into our lives
And became everyone's friend.

**Claire Miller  (15)**
Uplands School

# My T-Shirt

Sparkly,
Gently pastel
Strapless
Very girly

Bare neck, bare arms
To enjoy the sun's rays
Brown tummy revealed

Cool wash only
Spin dry, cool iron
Folded neatly in my room

Careful washing prevents colours
Fading too quickly
The wash rotates

Choosing a T-shirt
The colours, the size
Style and shape

Superb stitching
With sequins galore
Pink shiny beads, great

Silky round neck
On a rainbow background
Waist-length, short

Tight and skinny
The height of fashion!
The height of fashion!

We are models, we are
Tall, we are chic
And so stunning

Parading with pride
On top of the world
Step by step

Removing my T-shirt
Sending for wash
Tomorrow carefully selecting once more.

**Jennifer Grace Evans (11)**
Uplands School


# The Football Match

As I walk up the dirty stairway
I can see thousands of faces
Some familiar, some not
I look out onto the pitch
And see the footballers
Matching shirts as each other

Then the game begins
I can hear those ardent fans again
Shouting to cheer on their team
'Go on! Go on!' I shout
I'm cheering for the Blues
Tension is in the air
Which team will win?

Finally a goal is scored
My team has scored the winning goal
The fans are wild!
I can barely see the match
As everyone is on their feet
Cheering
1-0 to the Blues!
We won.

**Helen Day (13)**
Uplands School

# Boy Racer

Mazda, Rover
Honda, Subaru
Speeding noisily

Exhaust vibrating, engine revving
Release the clutch, spinning wheels
Tyres smoking

Lights go green
Hearts beating, adrenalin rush
Pink slips are held high

There's no turning back
The lights glimmer
As we pass

The Honda leads
Rover closing, Mazda third
I am waiting

Burning fuel
Surroundings are blurred
The Honda veers left

Sparks start flying
He hits the Mazda
*Bang! Crash! Bang!*

Nothing in it
As we speed on
As we speed on

We over-steer round the corner
Pushing to the limit
Neck and neck

Inject NOS
To take the lead
Final length home

Flag is in sight
Cross the line
And skid to a halt.

**Matthew Kelly (13)**
**Uplands School**

# Famous

Do I want to be famous
Like the kids on telly, should I act, sing or dance?
To rock and roll or croon for Pete, Foxy and Simon,
A formidable audition.

They must see my talent or my looks,
Can't forget my lines, must sing in tune.
It's my big chance, please God I can't blow it,
A good rendition would get me onto their books.

Fame and future, yes please,
TV films, fans, adoring of course.
Everything I've dreamt of depends on me now.
To impress these critics, hard nosed brow,
Will Nicky be on my side, please?

Hands damp, perspiration drips, all eyes and teeth smile,
The music intro starts now.
How much do I want this fame?
Let the melody wash over me,
Feel the beat!

It's all over, it went too quick, judgement day,
For me my song, yes, it's smiles and praise, I've won.
Original in tune, fantastic.
Good metaphors, praise, I can't get enough,
The blood, sweat and tears have paid off, *fame!*

**William Yeoman (13)**
**Uplands School**

# Paper

Paper, cold
Thin, whitely
Shaded brightly

In places, dimmer, darker
Quickly absorbing sun's
Warming glow

Getting warmer still
As day moves on
Reflecting sun's rays all around

More paper sits nearby
Tens, hundreds, thousands
Stacked so high

Machines to copy
Running, smoothing, running faster
Will paper last?

Teacher's copies
So many copies
Higher than machine. Now

Time to distribute
This heavily inked load
Gobbledy-gook, blurb

Important or not
A piece for all!
A piece for all!

Just a few more copies
Awaiting, dry and crisp
Heated by day

Expanding and moving
Day draws to a close
Paper gets cooler

Next day a boy
Turns fan on
Blow pushes all paper away.

**Lewis Tottle (11)**
**Uplands School**


# Valentine

Not a ring or a night out.

I give you a candle, it promises love,
It is wrapped in flowery paper,
Do you like it? It promises trust my dear,
Like the careful undressing of love, here light it.

Here take it, I hope you will keep it close,
It will blind you with its lights,
Like the sun its flame will shine through the night till morning,
It will shine on your complexion till dawn,
The flame will glimmer through the night.

I'm trying to be truthful,

Not a cute card or a teddy,

I give you a candle,
Its fierce scent will stay with you close,
Fierce and scentful, its scent will cling to you,
It will burn through the night till you wake,
For as long as we are two.

Take it, it is for you,
Its smoke will make a heart,
If you wish I shall recite a romantic poem,
Lethal its power, it could cause tears,
Its scent will cling to you, cling to your life.

**Jamie Bath (13)**
**Uplands School**

# Television

TV, very
Fun, sometimes,
Very sad

The remote seems to
Get further away from you,
It finally stops.

I grab it,
Hold it, keep it;
The small buttons look huge.

My finger insists on
Pushing the button,
It's now BBC2.

I hate BBC2,
It changes to BBC1.

It's CBBC,
Blue Peter's on,
Making a rocket. I

Write down objects,
That I will need,
Changing, the

Channel, it's ITV,
No, no, not ITV!
No, no, not ITV!

Neighbours is on, it's the
Worst, now it's BBC4,
It is OK.

It's time for
The eight o'clock news,
Nothing to watch:

I think I'm done,
I'm going upstairs,
I'll see you tomorrow, TV.

**Alistair Wilson  (11)**
Uplands School


# Valentine

Not a teddy or a box of chocolate,

I give you a knife,
It is a shooting star in a manufactured packaging,
It promises wishes,
Like the careful trust of love.

Here it will suppress you with pain,
Like a lover,
It will make your reflection a naïve photo of awkwardness.

I am trying to be truthful,

Not a singing card or a red rose.

I give you a knife,
Its sharp cuts will remind you,
Happiness and anger,
As we are,
For eternity as we are.

Hold it,
Its inconspicuous shape will seem tender,
If you prefer,
Lethal,
Its wounds will be inflicted on you,
Inflicted on us.

**Joe Mason  (13)**
Uplands School

# Torn Apart

The hours turned into days,
The days turned into months,
The same routine over
And over again.
Shovelling mud from here to there,
From there to here.
Adjusting the angle,
The depth,
The length,
The height.
All my time,
All my energy,
Put towards a heap of dirt.
Not just any heap of dirt,
My heap of dirt.
How long this went on for?
I do not know!
The only thing that I do know,
Is that is was worth it!
For the days that I had it,
Was a time of enjoyment,
Delight,
Satisfaction!

Little did I know,
That some being,
Some kind of *Satan,*
Could get the nerve to . . .
Drive a plough, straight,
Through the heart of *my* creation.
All my time,
Work,
Energy,
Love,
Being torn apart,
In front of my eyes,

I cannot describe to you,
The anger,
The hatred,
That I felt that day.

I sat in front of my ruined,
Work of art for about twenty minutes,
Contemplating on what I,
Had just experienced.
Then suddenly I bolted upright,
As if an energy wave had just,
Exploded, right in the heart of my soul.
I grabbed my shovel,
Walked over to the newly flattened ground
And started on something,
Bigger than ever before.

**Miles Rowbrey  (15)**
**Uplands School**


# Is This Love?

Did you ever realise what the funny feelings inside you were?

Everyone says they get butterflies,
But for different reasons,
Not everyone knows what they are or mean,
Do you?

I think the feelings inside are harmless,
But some people feel the pain.

Some people try hard to find this,
But what have they got to gain?

Love or lust,
Or is it all about trust.

No one ever knows if it's true,
But some people do.

**Ashley Thompson  (14)**
**Uplands School**

# The Pointless Cycle

The pointless cycle; constant
It continues without end,
On and on, daily, weekly, never stopping.
The uselessness of its contents,
Apparent only to some.

The un-resolute isochronism,
Never does it cease,
It continues vagrantly, purposelessly.
The cycle renewing itself unpreventably,
Automated, the system's mechanism.

The cycle creating; constantly
More preventions from itself,
Its values and beliefs compromised
From within. Compromised by those who would uphold them.
The un-resolute isochronism
Never does it cease.

**Peter Lucas  (15)**
**Uplands School**


# To Sail A Boat

To sail a boat
Whether it be to race, or just to go for a jolly!
To sail a boat is just such great fun!
From lasers to mirrors, or maybe even 420s,
It does not matter it's still such great fun to sail a boat.
During the summer sun, with the light sparkling on the water,
Like the twinkle of a star
Or during the frosty winter, with our wetsuits and boots,
In the freezing cold!
It does not matter it is still such great fun
To sail a boat,
That is!

**Tim Borrill  (14)**
**Uplands School**

# Two Sides Of The Wall

What is this world we live in about?
Past cannot be changed,
However, present and future can.

The goodness of life in this world is spread unevenly,
This uneven spread has lead to areas of weakness,
Dryness
And questions, which ask,

'Will an unfulfilled life, that doesn't know how people live on the other
side, be given a chance to live differently?'

So many questions,
So much time,
So many lives wasted.

Will a dry pallet be watered?
Will an empty stomach be filled?

Lives *can* change, but
*Will* lives change?

**Lucia Briant  (14)**
**Uplands School**


# The Summer Has Gone

The summer has gone for yet another year,
The early darkness in the evening has begun.
No more football for me at the park after 5:00,
My shorts and my sandals have been put away,
Out come the woolly hats, gloves and Wellingtons,
The only good thing about the summer going is . . .
The start of the new football season!

**Michael Harrison  (14)**
**Uplands School**

# The Coral

A pinnacle of jagged rock,
Able to take the souls of passers-by,
Willing or not,
This evil formation will endlessly exterminate.

As the inanimate monster lies,
Waiting for a visitor to come,
In an uncontrollable
Lust for a vengeance of the last.

No one survives,
Whether a victim or not,
The coral will fight,
Fight a selfish battle,
To allow one,
Allow a single survivor,
That is the coral itself.

Unaware that a film of mystery will always be present,
A film ever growing in size with each kill,
Each sunken ship and loss of life,
The coral will be submerged,
To itself and others.

**Sam Johnson  (14)**
**Uplands School**


# Life

Life is like a turn, you never seem to know what is round the corner
It is like a present that is wrapped full of surprises
Anxious to know what is inside
One minute we will love life but then again one minute we will hate it
Life is like a game that we would all like to win
Each and every one of our lives is unique and one in itself.

**Luke James  (14)**
**Uplands School**

# Alcohol

Alcohol is the stuff dreams are made of
It slows everything down and makes people look pretty
It gives you the feel of confidence and superiority
Nothing else matters apart from you and your drink
But it seems everybody's drunk apart from you
You start to talk to things, inanimate objects
Who become your best mates
And the journey to your place of destination seems like an adventure
But yet your dream turns to a nightmare when you
Wake up with a headache
And the slightest sound seems like someone banging you
On the head with a two by four
And you can't remember a thing
So you assume you had a good night.

**Edward Clarke (15)**
**Uplands School**


# The Silver Screen

The lights go down
The atmosphere and mood is set
What is to be expected?
A hush falls over the audience

The beginning scenes
Capture the audience's attention
Confined to a new world
Close-ups, zoom, flash-backs, glimpses

All too soon the credits roll
It's back to reality
The audience entertained most successfully
Until the next time your world has changed.

**Emma Mears (14)**
**Uplands School**

## My Poem

Monday again and English homework set as usual,
Write a poem, well it shouldn't be too hard,
Or so I thought, until I sat
And still I sat thinking about my poem.
Music! I shall write my poem about music!
And so I sat brainstorming thinking about my music poem.
Well it turned out quite hard,
Unfortunately so.
So I sat again thinking, thinking about my poem.
Pets! That's as good a subject as any!
So I sat again brainstorming, loads of ideas,
Or so I thought. Into the fourth line
And nothing left to say.
Yet again I found myself sitting, thinking about my poem.
Thinking what to write.
So here, I give it to you,
My poem. Not about music or pets,
Or anything in-between. This is my poem about my poem!
Weird how things work out, isn't it?

**Louis Bosence (14)**
**Uplands School**

## The Ship

The ship I was on all those years ago has just come back to life,
It has just risen again, it has just reminded me of the awful past,
I have just been reminded of what I don't want to know,
My friends,
My family,
They have all come back to me,
I don't want to remember,
Please don't come back,
Go back, stay there, leave me alone.

**Ryan Tottle (14)**
**Uplands School**

# The Ignorant Human

They are the kings of the land,
The terror of the seas.

They are oblivious to what they have brought upon this world,
Pollution, destruction, dying and distress.

They clash and the world trembles,
Buckles at the knees.

They perform religious rituals,
Believe in pointless things.

They are very trusting,
Therefore easily fooled.

They blunder on like blind men,
Not seeing what lies ahead.

They do not know their destinies,
But one day they'll find out.

**Jonathan Mills  (14)**
**Uplands School**


# Mooring Up

Before we moor up
The fenders out
Shout to the bow man
'Get ready'
We start to drift
He's deaf to the instruction
'Let go of the anchor!'
Disaster has struck!
An anchor line is around
The prop
We've crossed anchors
Mel dives below and hides
I shout 'Help'
And wonder what to do.

**Emma Bartlett  (15)**
**Uplands School**

# As I

As I pull the plug from the bath
I watch the water swirl away like a whirlpool
Wondering where the water will go to next
I think about all the unfortunate children
Who would jump at the chance for some water

As I slither down into my bed
Pulling the covers up around my neck
Snuggling up to my teddy and becoming warm
I think about homeless people all over the world
Who have nowhere to live or sleep.

As I watch people pile their plates with food
What looks like mountains happens to be some delicious meal
Then say they're not hungry when they have eaten a couple of
mouthfuls
I think about people who go for days
Without food and die of starvation.

As I write this poem I stop for a moment
And picture what is going on with the world,
I carry on writing and watching my pen flow across the page
I think about what we can do
To stop these crisis from occurring.

**Katie Creevy (15)**
**Uplands School**


# Memory

As I gaze into your eyes
I see a field of lush golden sunflowers
I feel the soft breeze pass through my hair

As I gaze once more I feel the burning sun hit down on my back
I hear the water of the lake flow
Then it became rain, I feel it hit upon my body
But soon the rain, the wind, the sun and the sunflowers
Disappear into the mist of your memory then it became a fog.

**Jenny Ricketts (13)**
**Uplands School**

# The Super Car

The colour,
Pearlescent yellow
Front and side
Air vents hint
At its great power

Huge circular exhausts
Pronouncing themselves
Out of the gently sloping
Rear of the  car
With a note
Like a roaring lion

Sport interior
With bucket seats
And leather trim

The engine
An American V8
Pumping out over
Four hundred horsepower.

**Guy Adams  (14)**
**Uplands School**


# Winter's Day

The snowflakes are falling, drawing closer, getting louder.
All that there is, is a silhouetted shape at the end of the field.
The snow sweeps the field like a white duvet sheet.
A set of paw prints run up to the pond,
Where a fox stands to watch the last leaf fall.
The fox is frightened then runs for his life
As the last leaf glides through the wind.
Falling and falling until it hits the ground.
Then you know it is a start of a cold winter's day.

**Alex Middleditch  (14)**
**Uplands School**

# Home

Home, shoes kicked off by the front door.
Coats hung on bentwood.
Mum shouts, 'Hi there, what's new?'
Everyone in the kitchen, lots of chatter.

Home, smells of dinner as usual,
Hungry people saying, 'When's it ready?'
Plates and glasses clatter on the table,
Everyone sat waiting for tea to begin.

Home, watching television, now exciting soaps,
All sat as a family with pyjamas on.
Pass the biscuits, drinks all around,
All of us sitting safe and sound.

Home, 'Time for bed,' she said, already?
I don't mind, I've had a busy day.
School is tiring up and down the stairs,
Happy under the duvet, warm as toast, home!

**Jessica Owens  (13)**
**Uplands School**


# The Haunting

A cold damp mist hangs below the dark murky sky at night,
Bats and strange creatures roam their territory,
A grandfather clock sounds,
The entrance gate's rusty hinges try to compete
With a repetitive screech,
You better leave now as the haunting is just beginning!

**Jennie Bird  (14)**
**Uplands School**

# A Photograph

What's a photograph?
An image of the past
A time gone forever
You can see everything
The memories of your own faded past
Or the past of a friend the way you've never seen them

Anger, pain and hurt
Even under a smile
Or the happiness, love and beauty
In a quick expression
It's all there

Why do we take photographs?
To remind us of what we thought of as the norm
Or to give the picture of how it once was
To show our past to the future.

**Sarah-Jane Foster  (15)**
**Uplands School**


# The Wind

The wind blows by
I feel it in my hair
I love the wind
I love the air

I walk through the park
The sun is in the sky
The wind has gone
The wind has come to die.

**James Creevy  (12)**
**Uplands School**

# The Girl

I see her there, looking at me,
Big blue eyes and long blonde hair,
I reach out my arm
And she does too,
But we never seem to touch.

Every day when I come home from school,
I see her standing there,
Always looking just as I am.
Sometimes her hair is tied up,
Sometimes in plaits or even messy,
Just like me.

If I say hello to her,
The words do not come out of her mouth,
Although she means to speak,
We can't really talk to each other,
She isn't sad, unless I am,
She can't see me although I can see her.

One day I came home from school
And she had gone,
So had my mirror.

**Rhiannon Wilson  (13)**
**Uplands School**


# The Shark

The shark is a streamlined killer gliding through the waves,
A lonely solitary figure swimming through the night.

As deadly as a knife, poised to strike and kill,
But as lonely as the darkness always standing still.

It kills to live and lives to kill but always for a reason
And when it dies, no one cries for the sorry story of a shark.

**Oscar Weiner  (13)**
**Uplands School**

# Riding My Bike

I go to gather my gear so I'm ready to go,
Jump on my bike and I travel onwards.
Weaving in and out of the pedestrians,
They don't know what happened, it was all too fast.
I feel the wind whip on my face,
Like daggers through the air, stabbing away.
I go to the car park to practise some tricks,
With my stunt pegs I grind down the banister.
Downhill is great, with gathering speed,
Just hope those brakes work, or I won't see my bike again.
I hop onto the pavement; I'm going to the shops,
Skid to the door and chain it up.
In no time at all, I have reached my destination,
I bought some sweeties for the journey home.
Hurtling down the road, I nearly hit my neighbour,
Whizzed through the gate, home at last.

**Tom Nicolet  (14)**
**Uplands School**


# My Cat

My beautiful black cat,
Sits patiently waiting and watching,
Crouching low muscles tense,
Eyes fixed upon the prey.

She crawls forward slowly,
Then waits until the right moment comes
And then, and only then does she pounce.

The mouse is pinned to the ground,
Still and stunned,
The cat seems to lose interest and releases her grip,
The mouse runs off and the game starts again.

**Toby Hoare  (12)**
**Uplands School**

# The Race!

The car sits behind the lights waiting for
Them to turn green
The car waits like a hungry tiger!
Pressure is building . . .

Red!

Amber!

Green!

The race has now begun! The car skids, sweeps and swerves
Round the track.
Triumphantly the car passes the finish line.
It sits there exhausted like a spider,
After spinning its web!

**Charlie Power (13)**
Uplands School


# Oscar

Every day I open Oscar's cage,
To see him smiling back at me,
He wakes up and waddles over to have a bite to eat,
I get him out and give him a groom,
Then I put him in his ball.
He runs like the wind, if he really can be bothered
And slows down to the speed of a snail,
He sits tight until I get him out
And when I do, he doesn't want to move,
So I give him another groom
And play with him for a bit,
Then I put him back in his cage
And say goodbye until tomorrow.

**Fleur Ruddick (13)**
Uplands School

# My Ride

I get on my horse
We start our journey
The horse starts to walk on the stony path
Clip-clop, clip-clop

Now we start to get faster
'Trot on Layla,' I said
I hang on tight
And start to count
'1-2, 1-2,' I whisper

But then I lose control of Layla
'Stop Layla,' I shout
I tried to pull on the reins
But she starts to canter
My feet come out of the stirrups
I start to slide out of my saddle
'Ouch!' I screamed
I get up and dust myself off
My journey starts again.

**Emily Daniels  (12)**
**Uplands School**


# World Peace

Why can't the world be peaceful?
Why does there have to be wars?
Is it because there's no friendliness?
Or is it just the way life goes?
Maybe one day my wish will come true
And the world will be a better place.

**Chloe Everett  (13)**
**Uplands School**

# Seasons Of The Sea

Radiant, vibrant, dancing,
Glistening ripples.
A vast expanse of perpetual motion.
Whirlpools left behind.

Shimmering colours,
Emerald, sapphire, aquamarine.
Sparkling like jewels in the sun.
Children identifying creatures in crystal clear water.

Dreams, tranquillity, thoughts,
Driftwood swept into the wearisome sand.
Changing colours.
Storm clouds muster like armies ready for battle.

Amethyst, grey, cold,
The sound of waves crashing.
Cannons firing, horses shying.
Abandoned nets, battered boats.
Deserted beach.

**Anastasia Hernandez Beaumont (12)**
**Uplands School**


# Red

Red is menacing and daring like the Devil
Red is also the colour of fire engines dashing to the rescue
Red is the colour of the prey after the predator has struck
Red is the colour teachers use to mark our work
Red is the colour that tells us to come to a halt
Red is the colour of the best team in the world, Manchester United
Red is the colour of blood, which we donate to others
Red is the colour of danger
Red is . . .

**Onari Tariah (12)**
**Uplands School**

# Winning

91:30 minutes gone,
You're 3-0 up,
No way back
For the other team.

92 minutes gone,
You're 3-1 up,
There might be
A way back for the
Other team.

4 minutes remaining,
They've scored again,
What's next 3-3?
Not if you can help it.

Maybe you couldn't,
The game's all-square,
You've got a corner,
Down you go.

It's coming to you,
Are you going to score
Or get pushed over?

*Bang*, it hits your head,
Off it goes,
Right into the net.

You're the winner,
Not just your team,
Because you can
Stand up proud and
Take the vow
That goal was *mine!*

**Sam Breslin (15)**
**Uplands School**

# Apple

Look, it's
A red
Lonely apple

It looks very tasty
It looks very shiny sitting
There by itself

Nobody knows it
It looks so succulent
I might just eat it

It looks a stunner
Round and big
Tasty and yummy

Even the colour
Makes me want to
Do you think?

I should
Or shall I just leave it?
My lips are sealed
My eyes are direct
I can't stand

It, I must
No, I must not!
No, I must not!

Oh one little bite
I can't ask my mum
She'll say no

Not my dad
Not even my brother
Nor my sister

I can't do it
Not even one
Bite, oops, I just did.

**Tim Johnson (11)**
**Uplands School**

# Storm

Storm, raging through
The night, crashing, booming

Watching, waiting, *crash! Bang!*
Listening, lighting up the trees like candles

Raining loudly, crying, downpour,
Buckets of water

Thunder, furious, mad, exploding,
Roaring through the night

Never stopping, angry, mad
No boundaries, no friends, just anger

Shouting and roaming
Angry with life, crying
And crying

Not caring, not thinking
Blindly raging its
Way through the night

Nothing can hide
Nothing is spared
From madness

And for what
What is left but wreckage?
Nothing but rubble and debris

Morning breaks
The storm abates
Peace is restored.

**Peter Gordon  (11)**
**Uplands School**

# Hallowe'en Poem

Hallowe'en is my favourite time of year,
It's a struggle getting ready . . .
We need to carve the pumpkins,
Don't forget the costumes,
What about the face paints?
Did you buy the sweets?
My devil horns?
My vampire teeth?
*What time is it?*
Hallowe'en is my favourite event.

Once we are ready and looking scary,
We grab the pumpkins and the sweet bags,
Walk out the door
And begin.
We work our way up the street,
Hallowe'en is my favourite event.

We creep to the first door,
Everyone's nervous.
We slowly knock at the door,
We wait in anticipation.
Then . . .
Suddenly . . .
'Hello'
'Trick or treat!'
The man rummaged in the bowl
We had toffee chews
Lollipops and loads more
Hallowe'en is my favourite event.

**Molly Bradshaw  (12)**
**Uplands School**

# The Sky

Daylight, very
Quietly, silently
Very still

The sun, the clouds
Take over from the darkness
With bright daylight

Everyone sees us
Loves us, wants us
Shining brightly in the sky

The rays from the
Sun shine brightly
Through the clouds

Even the birds
Flap wings, hawk loud
Twittering and chirping

A plane
Flies past loudly
Disturbs the peace, but

A breeze blows
On the appearance of
A rainbow with

Many bright colours
Colours of the rainbow!
Colours of the rainbow!

The colours shine, blue and
Red, green and yellow
Violet and indigo

People turn and
Glare at the sight
Marvellous and fantastic

The sky turns red
Rainbow dies down
The calm before the storm.

**Amy Gollings  (11)**
**Uplands School**

# Hats

Soft, snugly
Comfy, fluffy
Warm as toast

It's hard, it's stiff
It sits hard and uncomfortably
On my head

Everyone sees us
Red ones, blue ones
Ugly ones are not worn

Small hand insist on
Taking us off
The soft heads

Adjust the look
Tip it, twist it
Oh the perfection

Flower power
Or just plain
Whatever you like

We don't like water
It makes us soggy
Shrinking, floppy, not

Being looked after
People care, people don't
People care, people don't!

Hanging on hooks, in a
Box, in a heap
Placed with care

Trendy and cool
Or old fashioned and grannyfied
Everybody has one

We wear them morning
Noon and night
Hats we love to wear.

**Oliver Hoare  (11)**
**Uplands School**

# Windsurfing

I'm standing in the water,
The waves splashing against my waist,
My knee is on the board now,
I can do this!

Kneeling's not too difficult,
Once I have my balance,
Now I need to stand,
I can do this!

I'm standing on the board,
All wobbly and weak,
Trying to lift the mast,
I can do this!

The sail is heavy,
When full of water,
Will I get it up?
I can do this!

The sail is up,
The wind is catching,
I'm darting across the waves,
I really *can* do this!

Picking up speed now,
There's a storm coming in,
Going out to sea,
Should I do this?

Decided against it,
Coming back to shore,
The wind's still rising,
Can I do this?

Condor's wash is coming,
Closer by the second,
*Splash,*
*I can't do this!*

**Jonathan Cooper (12)**
**Uplands School**

# The Sea

The surface of the deep blue sea is a sheet of diamonds
As it shines brightly in the sun.
I jump in and the diamond sheet shatters like glass.
The water feels like velvet on my skin as I dive down into the beyond.

The tropical fish tickle my skin as I gaze at the sea bed below.
Sunlight filters through the sea to light the rainbow coloured reef.
I can hear the wonderful sound of the dolphins calling,
It is music to my ears.
As the dolphins glide past, they touch me and I feel their
                                        silky, soft skin.
I speed to explore the mysterious depths.
Fish and other amazing creatures swarm around the reef
Like a deadly group of wasps.
Jellyfish bop up and down like yo-yos.

Hidden under the reef is the lost city, all the jewels glow colourfully,
The huge pillars are as white as snow.
I take a further look into the peculiar temple,
Suddenly a great white shark appears!
My heart is racing . . . it's coming towards me!
I shoot off like a rocket,
I look behind me and I can see its jaws snapping like
                                        clamps behind me.
I swim as fast as I can and look behind me again,
I can see nothing, but can feel a soft liquid around me that
                                        feels like soap.
The dark liquid is now fading like the light in the sky.
I observe an opalescent, orange, octopus in the opaque ocean.

I float back up to the surface like a hot air balloon in the sky.
Passing the mysterious depths and the jewels that glare brightly
                                        in the lost city's temple,
I pass a huge blue whale covered with barnacles.

As I reach the surface, the light in the sky deteriorates as the sun sets
                                        into the ocean.

The sea.

**Jack Kane  (13)**
**Uplands School**

# Family

Family is homely, it is very
Much like a net, stray, but little and will
The net break? Will the strong bond fall
Well, with it? What will be there to support it?
Who would believe why the bond would break well why?

Family is warm like a hot bath,
It is the home where life began
And where love and faithfulness is spawned, it is also where
Children play and laugh and adults are smiling,
I wish my family was like that.

Family is a welcome mat,
Welcoming you, with open arms,
It also greets you with a beaming smile,
Look at the children who are smiling,
Look at them all laughing and joking.

Family is a pot,
Where eternal life and
Love, gratitude and faithfulness spread throughout all
That love will hopefully stay,
Family is a commitment to joy.

Family is a mattress, it is soft,
It is bouncy, it is warm keeping you safe,
Danger, misery and woe gone,
Family is home, it is comfort,
Peace of mind, comforting and God for life.

**Nabil Mahmoud  (13)**
**Uplands School**

# My Favourite Place To Be

My favourite place to be
Is many miles away.
I wish I could go every week,
But I mustn't push my luck.

When I get near I
Start to twitch anxiously.
I'm so excited, I start to daydream
About all the wonderful thrills.

The ride starts, we shake
In our seats, rocketing
Along the twisted, winding rails, screaming loudly!
Hanging upside-down, we drop

I wake up, I'm on
An aeroplane, we are
Nearly there, I can't sleep so instead
I decide to eat lunch

But what do I eat?
Nothing, I fall asleep
I had just began to dream peacefully . . .
When *bang* the aeroplane landed

'Yes!' I shouted, I am
Here at last, my
Favourite place to be, have you guessed
It yet? It's . . .
*Florida!*

**Roxanne Coulstock  (11)**
**Uplands School**

# Valentine

Not a gold ring or a teddy bear.

I give you an orange.
It is a sun wrapped in orange paper.
It promises light,
Like the careful undressing of love.

Here.

It will blind you if you open it incorrectly,
Like a lover.
It will make your face orange
With its powers.

I am trying to be fair.

Not a funny card or some delicious chocolates.

I give you an orange,
Its thirst-quenching taste will stay on your lips,
Attractive and attacking,
As I am,
For as long as you want.

Have it.
Its segments for each part of
Our relationship,
Lethal.
Its taste will cling to your lips,
Cling to your fingers.

**Peter Dixon  (13)**
**Uplands School**

# Love

Not perfume or a gold ring
I give you a clock, is it eternity?
Or is it our blossoming love
Does it freeze your heart? Like the ticking clock
Is our love like the blooming rose in the springtime?

I will always love you forever
Concealed behind glass, it is time
Its hands will grab at your soul forever more
Our love will keep on burning like a candle
It will give you infinite

It is time in itself
Our love for each other, cherished
All we will ever need is each other
Like a boyfriend's love for his soul mate
I am trying to be loving

This clock is valuable
And quite precious to me
Like the hours we are together for evermore
Like our ever burning love.

Kind and giving, this is our love,
Better than a teddy, better than perfume.
Go on touch it, it's not lethal,
As we are, for as long as we are.
Not a mixed tape, fancy perfume, a clock.

**Piers Bate  (13)**
**Uplands School**

# Quick Hug From Mum

There you are,
Just been born,
Held in your mother's arms.

There you are,
Just turned three,
Just entering playschool,
But right before,
Need some reassurance,
Quick hug from Mum.

There you are,
Just turned five,
Starting school,
Don't know anyone,
Need some reassurance,
Quick hug from Mum.

There you are,
Just turned sixteen,
Finished school,
Starting work,
In the real world,
Need some reassurance,
Quick hug from Mum.

There you are,
Just turned twenty,
Started a family,
Stressed out from kids,
Need some reassurance,
Quick hug from Mum.

There you are,
Just turned thirty-eight,
Watching your child,
Nervously go to playschool,
You stop him,
Call him over,
Quick hug from Mum.

**Alexander Boucouvalas  (14)**
**Uplands School**

# My Bike

Blue, yellow, orange and very red is my bike
Smoothly, slyly it goes by
Very silently

Its handles don't allow sweat
To my brother on my bike I could've crept
When I cycle down the street, you will rarely hear a noise

Nobody can stop me
Just try, try to catch me
All wildlife leaves hastily

It is so shiny
Ever so finely
My bike will not cease to shine

Even the brakes
Are the best, they're made precisely
Ever so scratchless

Perfectly perfect
Enlarge the road
Let my bike through

It lives in oil
I love my bike
My bike rocks

My bike is great
My bike is excellent
My bike is excellent

Its silent brakes, its anti-sweat handles
The sly wheels
The silent bike

Wheels and chains, handles, saddles
My bike
Has no rust

I'll win bike competitions
We'll be first
We are waiting for competitions.

**Thomas Hawkins  (11)**
**Uplands School**

# The Sea Sponge

Deeply, very
Darkly, silently,
Peacefully still.

Our bodies, our crevices,
Provide shelter for the creatures,
From dangerous predators.

Our soft carpet,
Glows vividly, tangles chaotically;
While sea creatures graze lightly.

Long fingers stretching out,
Towards the surface,
Touching passing prawns,

Domain of predators.
Sea slugs, sea stars,
Common spiky urchins,

Completely relaxed,
Softened worn holes,
Water flowing through. We

Have no mouths,
No guts for digesting,
Breathe and reproduce

By pumping water.
The water is tasty!
The water is tasty!

We are cleaners, we are
Shelter, we are food,
We are healers.

Chemicals and toxins
We leak from ourselves.
For bad taste:

With these we shall
Treat human disease
And they will protect us.

**Terry Baskett  (11)**
**Uplands School**

# Misty Forest

In the forest, very scary
Whispers, very quiet
Also getting dark

Wind and lighting
Frightening
Why be scared?

Trees falling
Can't get away
Leaves are falling

Bark is ripping
Coming off
To make soul

The forest shall grow
Forever
Nature is large.

**William Brown (11)**
**Uplands School**


# The Crash

Window smashing, heart racing
The uneven battle between car and motorbike

In the aftermath they find a body
In the road
Still and silent

The survivor staggers street-wards
Shocked to witness the carnage

Lights flashing
Sirens blaring
Senses fading
Doors slam shut.

**Alanna Hamilton (12)**
**Uplands School**

# My Dog Is My Best Friend

*(In loving memory of my best friend, my dog, Bobby)*

I love my dog, I love my dog,
My dog is my favourite friend,
He sleeps with me at night,
He plays with me during the day,
Oh how I love my dog.

When I go to school,
I really miss my dog.
When I go to school,
I wish I could take him with me,
But I know I can't!

I love taking my dog for a walk in the park,
I have so much fun playing games,
Watching him dig and fetch a stick.

My dog eats three meals a day,
He loves his meat and vegetables,
Especially his tasty treats!

I dread the day,
When he dies,
Leaves me alone,
Standing in the park,
With just a lead in my hand,
With no one to lead me.

**Jace Latore  (14)**
**Uplands School**

# Valentine

Not a platinum ring or a silver necklace.

I give you a pen,
It is a water fountain overflowing.
It promises imagination,
Like the first moment of love.

Here.
It will express your feelings,
Like a lover.
It will make you write your story,
A story you dread to tell.

I am trying to be open.

Not a cuddly teddy bear or a hug.

I give you a pen,
Its endless motion will stay on your paper.
Longwearing and bright,
As we are.
For as long as we are.

Share it, its gold nib writes at a church.
If we choose,
Determined.
Its power will astonish you,
Astonish your paper.

**Abigail Langley  (13)**
**Uplands School**

# Sweet Chocolate

Milk chocolate is heaven
The pearly-cream stairs, the brown gates, is it love?
Milk, added to make it creamy
Melted in your hand, lick it off or wash it?
Sticky on your fingers forever will it last?

Dark chocolate as black as tarmac
The devil itself, or brown bliss
Purely indulgence, nobody wants to share their bar
Scoff it by yourself or share it with a friend
Either way it must be eaten

White chocolate, love it
As creamy as this pace, whitewash
Cream, cream and yet more cream, luxurious
Milky bar to Lindt, we love them all
It's absolutely gorgeous, mmmm

Chocolate being
Melted in the machine
The crunchy biscuits on the long conveyer belt
Smothered in milk chocolate
Being packed being wrapped in gold paper

Instructions how to eat your chocolate
Take off the gold paper, shove it in your mouth
Savour the taste, indulge in it
The sweetness, the warmth of a bar of chocolate
The creaminess, the rich brown blocks, heaven.

**Jack Hayter (13)**
**Uplands School**

# Ski-Tastic!

I stood all kitted out, ski suit, gloves, hat and all,
Waiting in anticipation amid the starkness of bright glistening snow,
Where the mountains seemed to stretch into infinity,
And the constant droning of the cable cars climbing
Higher and higher, like steps into the sky,
*Splish slosh* went the sound of my skis,
As I hoped I wouldn't fall to my knees.

Reaching the mountainous summit, little specks and dots
                                    were all I perceived,
My stomach churned over like a washing machine, trepidation
                                    filled my bones,
Scared! My eyes increased to the size of dinner plates,
My heart pumping faster and faster as I peered down the slope,
Then with a little jump -
*Splish slosh* went the sound of my skis,
As I hoped I wouldn't fall to my knees.

The silent slush of snow, like a knife slicing through a fresh lettuce,
Cold fresh air piercing my face, even the hairs on my nose froze,
As I weaved like a serpent down the slippery slope,
Knees trembling as if they were leaves on a tree on a windy day,
Travelling the speed of light, a feeling of great exhilaration
                                    swept through my body,
As I finally conquered my descent,
*Splish slosh* went the sound of my skis,
But, now I knew, I wouldn't fall to my knees.

**Louis Hashtroudi (11)**
**Uplands School**

# Aeroplane

Aeroplanes sore through the sky,
Like a kite, caught in the wind,
Like a bird heading south,
Through the wind and the rain,
Through storms and clouds,
Through sunny skies and perfect weather,
Aeroplanes are always to be found.

Aeroplanes are used for many things,
Such as travel or military use,
Or training, or just for fun,
Aeroplanes are everywhere
And always to be found.

**Tristan Breslin  (12)**
**Uplands School**


# The Car Crash

Like two beasts coming into battle
They charge with a sound like thunder
People fleeing, running
Trying to escape
Yells, cries and screams and then
Silence . . .

The grass is damp with blood
The realisation hits people
The beasts lay motionless
Alone . . .

**Harriet Tombs  (12)**
**Uplands School**

# A Boy

His smile is like the sun peeping through a dark rain cloud
With eyes as blue as the ocean and hair the colour of corn
He has long gangly legs and feet that he hasn't quite grown into yet
His hands are small but plump as a chicken's breast
He's kind
I rather like him but you've probably guessed that already
He stands out from all the rest and
That's why I like this
Boy!

**Bethany Williams (11)**
Uplands School


# Maraf

Its neck is as tall as a redwood,
It eats as much as a pig,
Its skin is as red as blood
And the eyes as brown as mud,
It is amazingly strong
And can even break down the strongest gate,
Its head is like a ram's
And when it gets angry
It destroys a gate or eats a plate.

**Andrew Houlder (11)**
Uplands School


# Sharky

He's black and smooth,
He frightens the people by thousands,
His prey so small.

His eyes so big,
His tail so long,
If you're not careful, you might be inside.

**William Smith (11)**
Uplands School

# Mums

It's not fair, Mum's always telling you what to do;
'Don't pick your nose,' 'Stand up straight,' 'Comb your hair,'
It's all the same;
'Get dressed,' 'Do this, do that,'
'Mushy peas for tea,'
Can't we ever do what *we want?*

**Christina Guerra-Unwin  (11)**
Uplands School

# Crocodilicus

His pointed nose
His rounded eyes
His razor teeth
Beneath the ice
His prey is poisoned
And ripped apart
He even eats the bloody heart!

**James Smith  (11)**
Uplands School

# Scoops

His sharp, pointed nose,
His dark and gloomy eyes,
His wings are so long and unique,
He kills his prey in a glimpse,
He goes fast as a rocket
But quiet as a mouse.

**Shadman Chowdhury  (10)**
Uplands School

# The School Team

I sit in the classroom waiting to hear,
Mr Low shouts, 'Go on, get out of here.'

We shot out of the door like lightning on legs.

To enter the playground for this big event,
For we have a football match between Year 7.

I know I will beat them,
I must, I will, I can survive.

We charged on the playground,
Like raging rhinos in a field.

They will likely to be killed,
When we won 5-1,
We all yelled, 'The battle is won.'
They replied, 'It's just begun.'

**Christian Bulpitt  (12)**
**Uplands School**


# The Monkey

The monkey swings from tree to tree,
It can climb from bottom to top,
I wish I was a monkey,
I would swing from tree to tree,
Hang upside down and glaze all day,
Never get told off,
I would not need to go to school,
Could eat just what I liked,
The only downside that I know
Is being prey to humans or big cats,
I wonder what you want to be,
I'm sure it's good, but won't beat me!

**Byron Russell  (10)**
**Uplands School**

# Family

Family is the most important thing,
Family are there to support you.
Our families love us,
We should cherish every moment
That we have with them.
Our family help us through life,
Whatever happens they are there for us,
Through difficult times they're there.
We should respect what they do and support them,
I will love my family forever!

**Dale Beesley  (10)**
**Uplands School**


# Branded A Freak

She knows what it is to be scared,
With emotions and feelings left unbarred.
Overhears teasing and feels attacked,
Into a corner, she seems to be backed.
Surprised, hurt and fighting her past,
Getting out of this place, leaving at last.
She can't wait to be gone, been branded a freak,
All of her life has been so bleak.
Eighteen at last and leaving this town,
No one left now to get her down.
She doesn't know why she's been treated this way,
Bullied and teased from the very first day.
Now that she's gone, the pain has stopped,
But into the lake her body has dropped.

**Rebecca Galton  (14)**
**Wentworth College**

# Silent Scream

A girl sits, staring
Avidly into space
She's thinking of the past
You can see it on her face
The shadows to her are dancing
Black and white are one
And in the dance come pictures
Of what she's seen and done
Her tortured mind is screaming
With guilt and twisted fear
The memories, they taunt her
But none of them are clear
The old crimes she committed
The people that she killed
For she once was a soldier
Committed and highly skilled
But shellshock, it has claimed her
It took her from the front
Her body looks almost normal
Her mind must bear the brunt
So now she just sits, staring
Avidly into space
She's thinking of the past
You can see it on her face.

**Pippa Janssenswillen (13)**
**Wentworth College**